LUX IN LUMINE

Essays to Honor W. Norman Pittenger

Edited by R. A. Norris, Jr.

 THE SEABURY PRESS, NEW YORK

Acknowledgment

Grateful acknowledgment is made to the following publisher for permission to quote copyrighted material from the title listed: Alfred A. Knopf—H. L. Mencken, *Mencken on Music: A Selection by Louis Cheslock.* Copyright 1926 by Alfred A. Knopf, Inc.; renewed 1954 by H. L. Mencken.

Contents

iii

The Contributors

LAWRENCE ROSE, S.T.D., Dean of the General Theological Seminary, New York City

HARVEY H. GUTHRIE, JR., TH.D., Professor of the Old Testament at the Episcopal Theological School, Cambridge, Massachusetts

JOHN KNOX, PH.D., D.D., Baldwin Professor of Sacred Literature at the Union Theological Seminary, New York City

E. V. N. GOETCHIUS, PH.D., TH.D., Professor of Biblical Languages at the Episcopal Theological School, Cambridge, Massachusetts

ROWAN A. GREER III, PH.D., Chaplain of the Edinburgh Theological College, Edinburgh, Scotland

R. A. NORRIS, JR., M.A., D.PHIL. (Oxon.), Associate Professor of Church History and Historical Theology at the Philadelphia Divinity School, Philadelphia, Pennsylvania

JAMES E. GRIFFISS, PH.D., Professor of Theology at the Episcopal Theological Seminary of the Caribbean, San Juan, Puerto Rico

L. G. PATTERSON, PH.D., Associate Professor of Church History at the Episcopal Theological School, Cambridge, Massachusetts

KENNETH J. WOOLLCOMBE, M.A. (Oxon.), S.T.D., Principal of the Edinburgh Theological College; Canon of St. Mary's Cathedral, Edinburgh, Scotland

JOSEPH FLETCHER, S.T.D., Robert Treat Paine Professor of Christian Social Ethics at the Episcopal Theological School, Cambridge, Massachusetts

WILLIAM H. RALSTON, S.T.M., Assistant Professor of the Philosophy of Religion and Ethics at the School of Theology of the University of the South, Sewanee, Tennessee

DURSTAN R McDONALD, S.T.B., Teaching Fellow in Religious Thought at the University of Pennsylvania, Philadelphia

iv

Preface

The essays in this volume have been collected to honor Professor
W. Norman Pittenger on the occasion of his departure from the
General Theological Seminary in New York City, where he has
been a member of the faculty for some thirty years. They are
not only a tribute to a man of broad and deep scholarship, a
theological thinker of exceptional clear-mindedness and honesty,
but also, and above all, a tribute to a teacher whose uncanny
ability to inform, inspire, and liberate the minds of those working with him has made him the moral creditor of three generations of students. None of those who have enjoyed his instruction
can be anything but thankful for the gracious and careless gen-
erosity with which he has habitually spent the learning and wit
garnered in a lifetime's study and reflection.

This book is therefore a token payment of an immense collective debt. Needless to say, not everyone who would have
wished to contribute to the volume was able to do so. The essays
included are, in the truest sense, tokens. The writers represent
a host of the friends, colleagues, and former students of Professor
Pittenger; and the diversity of topics to which they address themselves will suggest the range and variety of the interests which
he has pursued for himself and encouraged in others. At the
same time, the existence of this volume will bear witness to a
widespread sense of deprivation which many will feel at the dis-
appearance from their midst of a source of wisdom and counsel
on whose availability they have been accustomed to depend.

The Editor wishes to express his profound thanks to those

persons and institutions whose interest and assistance made the publication of this volume possible: Christ Church, Bronxville, New York; the Divinity School of the Protestant Episcopal Church in Philadelphia; the Reverend William A. Eddy, Jr.; the Episcopal Theological School, Cambridge, Massachusetts; the General Theological Seminary of the Protestant Episcopal Church; the Reverend Francis C. Huntington; the Very Reverend Ledlie I. Laughlin, Jr.; E. Townsend Look, Esq.; the Right Reverend Paul Moore, Jr.; the Reverend Robert R. Spears, Jr.; Trinity Parish, Princeton, New Jersey; and the Reverend Alan C. Tull. A particular word of gratitude is owing also to The Seabury Press, whose patient and enthusiastic cooperation in this project has made the tribute which it bears their own.

R. A. NORRIS, JR.

Philadelphia
January, 1966

W. Norman Pittenger—*An Appreciation*

BY DEAN LAWRENCE ROSE

One of W. Norman Pittenger's teachers, writing in the year 1935, set down as the task of the theological school: "the preparation of men to proclaim with power to each successive generation in its own tongue the good news of God." It was in that same year, while he was still an undergraduate, that Norman Pittenger was appointed a Tutor at the General Theological Seminary and began the teaching career that has, with many generations of students, worked mightily to fulfill the aim expressed in those words. As Fellow and Tutor until 1945, Instructor in Christian Apologetics from 1945 to 1951, and as Professor ever since, he has devoted his great gifts with singular concentration to the enlistment of his students in the Christian theological enterprise with a view to their persuasive presentation and interpretation of the Gospel.

These thirty years of teaching have been characterized by a prodigious energy. Whether in classroom instruction, seminar leadership, individual tuition or, what he has perhaps loved best, the give and take of quite informal groups, he has been unstinting in placing his enormous learning, extensive reading, and phenomenal memory at the disposal of his students. For along with his wide-ranging scholarship, along with his absorbing pursuit of understanding in theology, philosophy, science, and literature has been an intense concern for human beings and a capacity for friendship that has made his relationships with his students a vitalizing personal interchange.

His ministry has by no means been confined to the Seminary,

1

nor to that branch of the catholic Church that claims his devoted allegiance. On college campuses throughout the length
and breadth of this country, and in England, Canada, the Caribbean lands, Australia, Japan, and the Philippines, he has presented his witness to God in Christ as the "heart and centre of
Christianity" with rare sensitivity to contemporary and local
idiom. And he has shown himself equally at home with young
men and women in colleges, to parish clergy, groups of theologians, scholars in other disciplines, and just people. Few theologians
of our time, moreover, have contributed so much by way of the
written word to an understanding of the Christian message and
way of life in their power to illuminate and redeem the whole of
human experience. Many of his writings have been "popular" in
the best possible sense of the word—for people—designed to
bring the truth of Christianity out of the cloister or the study
and give it currency in the living thought of men and women
today. But not a few have taken their place in the first rank of
serious scholarly interpretations of Christian doctrines; among
these his contribution to the Library of Constructive Theology,
published in 1959 under the title *The Word Incarnate,* has to be
counted among the foremost studies in Christology of modern
times.

Dr. Pittenger served for twenty-three years as Chaplain to
the Guild of Scholars of the Episcopal Church; he was for some
time Vice-President of the Church Congress; and, long a member of the American Theological Society, he was for a term its
President. Ecumenical affairs, too, have occupied his attention
and his ardent interest: whether by way of his membership on
the Standing Commission on the Church and Social Problems
of the National Council of Churches; or on the Study Commission of the World Council of Churches; or in his capacity as
Vice Chairman since 1954 of the North American Section of the
Theological Commission of the World Council. In all these
spheres of service, as in his teaching and writing, he has striven

to bear witness at once to the catholic substance of the Christian faith and to the truth revealed in science and the humanities.

The essays contributed to this book in honor of Dr. Pittenger fall into two groups: one dealing with the Christian understanding of Jesus Christ, and the other with the relation between the Christian faith and modern culture. This is most appropriate, for in his own work as scholar, thinker, and teacher, these two matters have ever been among the main foci of his concern. In an essay published in 1939, he addressed himself to the "Christian interpretation or evaluation of the fact of Christ" and how we may arrive at it.[1] In the introduction to his first book, also dated 1939, he wrote: "In this small volume the attempt is made to see the power and presence of the divine Reality, and his ceaseless creative activity, in the whole range of life." [2]

Thus in one way or another all that Norman Pittenger has ever taught or written can be related, on the one hand, to the person of Jesus Christ in whom "the supreme Reality makes his most direct approach to the lives of men" [3] and, on the other, to his passionate conviction that Christian theology has to do not simply with a special religious experience, but with God in relation to the whole creative process and the totality of human experience. And it may be said that it is precisely the centering of his thought in Christ that has inspired in him, and in those who have learned from him, a generous openness to truth from any source, hospitality to new insights, and joy in life, human and divine.

1

Israel, Pagan Culture, and Biblical Theology

BY HARVEY H. GUTHRIE, JR.

It is widely accepted today that the distinctive faith of ancient
Israel found its earliest and most formative expression in the
confessions and institutions of a tribal amphictyony occupying
north-central Palestine in the two centuries preceding the establishment of the Davidic monarchy.[1] Some hold that Israel's self-
consciousness as a people under the sovereignty of the God
Yahweh developed only on the soil of Palestine as the traditions
of various, originally separate, elements in the amphictyony became related to one another in a common credo.[2] Others contend
that Israel's communal self-consciousness was the result of the
connected experiences of a group forming the nucleus of the
later, larger tribal league.[3] For those holding both views, however, the premonarchical amphictyony and its traditions and faith
figure importantly. Indeed, it is the fashion in contemporary interpretation of the Old Testament to define "Israel" in terms of
that amphictyony, to take the faith and institutions of the amphictyony to be the normative canon by which all later developments in Israel's life and religion are to be evaluated, and to
pass a negative theological judgment on motifs brought into her
faith and literature in the centuries following the establishment
of the monarchy under David and Solomon.[4]

What is centrally characteristic of and unique in the Israelite point of view undoubtedly took its origin in the period
of the amphictyony. It was then that the experiences of the various constituent parts of the amphictyony were related to one

another and to the central faith that the destiny of Israel was explicable only in terms of the active presence of Yahweh in her history. It is also true that to define Israel's theology solely or essentially in terms of what preceded the monarchy is to over-simplify the data supplied by Israel's history and by the Old Testament literature.[5] Both the classical prophets and the writers of the New Testament lacked the advantage of having read the Alt-Noth reconstruction of Israel's early history as well as the contemporary theologies of the Old Testament so dependent upon that reconstruction. Indeed, in spite of what contemporary scholarship tends to adjudge central to Israel's faith, the prophets and the New Testament employ heavily terms taken into Israel's vocabulary only after the age of the amphictyony had passed—"messiah" being the most obvious one. The location of "Israel," therefore, exclusively in the period preceding the monarchy is inadequate in terms of sheer historical fact. Further it can result in a grossly oversimplified theology in which the witness of the prophets, of Jesus, and of Paul, to the continuing action of the sovereign God in ongoing history is supplanted by a newer kind of propositional position in which orthodoxy and salvation are defined in terms of the intellectual apprehension and institutions of one age in the past. This is as untrue to what modern scholar-ship has revealed of the biblical point of view as were older propositional theologies.

This problem, which has emerged precisely because of the irrefutable advances of post-Wellhausen Old Testament scholar-ship, is the background against which this paper is written. What follows is but a caveat entered in the form of the statement of three facts. These facts, although obvious, are deserving of more stress than is usually given them.

I

First, it is a fact that the Philistines accomplished what they set out to do *vis à vis* the Israelite amphictyony toward the end of the eleventh century B.C., i.e., to break up the amphictyony. When the Israelite hosts had been routed and Saul and his sons lay dead on Mount Gilboa, "Israel" also was dead, existing only in the memory of those who had formed her. The ark, resting near the Philistine cities where the conquerors could easily keep track of it, was no longer borne before the Israelite armies in holy war or enshrined in a central sanctuary at which the tribes celebrated the amphictyonic festivals. Israel could be spoken of now only by recounting a story that had ended with Saul. The word no longer denoted a living, empirical reality.[6]

Some few years later—following the successes of David, first during the period of his kingship in Judah and then when he was recognized as king by all the tribes of the former amphictyony[7] —the scattered remnants of what had been Israel once again found themselves part of a living, empirical entity. This new entity, however, was far from being coterminous with or exactly like the old. While its ideology and official religion drew heavily upon the traditions and faith of the earlier Israel, it included other significant elements such as Judah and its constituent parts,[8] as well as the Edomite, Moabite, Ammonite, and Aramean kingdoms. Furthermore, the Jebusite city-kingdom of Jerusalem with its own ancient and strong traditions was the center from which David exercised his kingship. Those circles, descended from the central elements in the older Israel in which such things as the Elijah legends and the E document and Deuteronomy originated, never forgot that very formative influences in the life and religion of the new, Davidic Israel came from places other than the faith and traditions of the old amphictyony.[9] When the Philistine onslaught—in the face of which Saul represented only the final, tragic resurgence of the old spirit of the amphictyony—was finished, the "glory" had indeed departed from Israel. The "glory" returned only when Israel came to life again as part of a new Near Eastern city-kingdom and empire created by David.[10] Israel's faith and ancient traditions were once again preserved and proclaimed as the explanation of the existence of a living entity, but now in the setting of the Temple and cult and mythology of such a kingdom.

Through the two centuries of her existence as an amphictyony in Palestine, the older Israel apparently had refused to have anything to do with just such a Temple and cult and mythology. Premonarchical Israel's view of God, man, and the human problem had been very different from that of the ancient Near Eastern world in general.[11] The basic political unit of that world was the city-kingdom, the focus of what, in modern terms, would be called the religious and the political aspects of life. Around the city lay the cultivated fields and, beyond them, the "wilderness." At the center of the city stood the palace-Temple complex, the place where the human realm made contact with the heavenly, from which the order of the heavenly realm radiated out into the human realm. In the worship of the Temple, led by the priest-king himself on the more important occasions, the community sought properly to relate itself to the gods in whom the forces, good and evil, upon which life was dependent were personified. In the recital of the cosmic myth and in mimetic cultic action the gods with whose existence and activity life was bound up were acknowledged. The chief figure of the pantheon, the "high god" of the particular place, was hailed as the ruler under whose power the various other gods were kept in check and made to serve the maintenance of life, order, and well-being. Epic myths recounted how he had won the victory that had resulted in this state of things and had brought into being the world in which men lived. As the "high god" continued to manifest his sovereignty by the continuance of order in the natural universe and by prospering the fortunes of his earthly vicegerent, the king, life and order prevailed over death and chaos in the people's existence.

Such was the basic pattern.[12] It could be extended to various outlying cities as "daughters" of the city-kingdom that was the center of power in an area. It might also be extended into a huge empire including a large number of city-kingdoms, in which the "high gods" of subject places had to acknowledge their subordination to the "high god" of the central city. The city-kingdom, however, was the basic unit, and even the empire would continue to bear the name of the city-kingdom from which imperial power was wielded, Ashur or Babylon or whatever it might be. Such a pattern was characteristic of civilization in the ancient Near East. Indeed any god worthy of the name presided from such a place and in such a way over his territory and his people, and this reflected the way in which he presided over the great assembly of the gods whose subduer and leader he was. Furthermore any people that was, to put it colloquially, at all a "somebody" in the ancient world lived in terms of such a pattern and ordered its life in terms of such a view of things.

Israel's point of view, however, was different. The clan and tribal groups constituting the premonarchical amphictyony were thoroughly convinced that the locus of meaning for them lay in the series of historical events that had brought them into self-consciousness as a people and into possession of the territory they occupied in Palestine. Their relationship, therefore, with Yahweh their God did not have primarily to do with the phenomena of the physical universe, with the round of the seasons or the fertility of the soil, crucial to the existence of finite man and central to the cult and mythology of the ancient Near East. Because Yahweh had called them to be his people before their identity was bound to one geographical area, had commanded and guided and fought for them in the area of historical action and decision, the fundamental issues of existence lay, for them, in their involvement in a communal, historical context in which they were responsible participants.

Thus Israel's mythos was fundamentally different from that of the peoples around her.[13] It did not locate the issues of existence in what transpired or had transpired before the beginning

of time, in the realm of the gods, in a cosmic drama mirrored in
the recurrent cycle of nature. It was a mythos locating the issues
of existence in what had transpired, in what was transpiring, in
the empirical history in which she was involved as a people. Her
mythos took the form of a credo, a recital of those events through
which she had come to her present status and in which she had
come to know her God.[14] It was quite unlike those mythological
accountings for the presence of order and stability in the world
of nature which figured centrally among her contemporaries.
Yahweh was the personification of no natural force or phenomenon, and his presence was not primarily manifest in such forces
and phenomena. To tell who he was necessitated dealing with
remembered events rather than with mythical occurrences outside the cosmos as man knew it.[15] The locus of meaning lay in
the history which had brought man to his given present and in
which he continued to play a significant role.

The results of such a theology and anthropology were, for
Israel, expressed in the concept of the covenant which was the
basis of her communal life.[16] Just as a relationship between two
persons is structured by the character of the persons in the relationship, so the nature of Israel's life was determined by the
character of Yahweh. The structure was the covenant, defined
in the apodictic "words" and the casuistic application of the
"words" in statutes and ordinances, which constituted the "law"
by which Israel lived under Yahweh.[17] Given the character of
Yahweh and her experience of life under him, the fundamental
nature of things could not, for Israel, be drawn in mythology of
the usual kind. It had to be expressed in what, anachronistically,
were political rather than religious terms. This is made clear in
recent studies in the origins of covenant and law that show how
the covenant *Gattung* underlying the amphictyony's expression
of the structure of its relationship with Yahweh originated in the
suzerainty treaties granted to subject states by the Hittite em-
perors.[18]

It could be argued that such a sacral polity was congenial to nomads or seminomads for whom the issues of life were not tied to specific places or the natural forces so important to settled, agrarian societies. It is nevertheless true that, whereas innumerable groups of nomadic and seminomadic peoples entered the arable areas of the fertile crescent and took on the civilization and religion common to it, Israel remained steadfastly loyal to her own faith and institutions for two hundred or more years after her settlement of Palestine. Others might become "somebodies" by taking over territories and the common religio-political pattern,[19] but it was precisely this that the Israelite tribal confederation refused to do from the obscure beginnings of its occupation of Palestine through two centuries of existence and growth. Furthermore G. E. Mendenhall has recently argued most compellingly that Israel's covenant polity may not have been left over from nomadic days at all, but may have been the basis of a conscious revolution against and withdrawal from the prevailing social order of the ancient Near East.[20]

So powerful was Israel's conviction of the sovereign authority of Yahweh in the realm of events and of her own covenant obligation to him, and so firm was her faith with regard to her destiny under him, that she refused to appropriate for herself any cosmogony locating the issues of human existence elsewhere than in the historical area upon which Yahweh's sovereignty had been seen to impinge and in which Israel's covenant obligations were central. To do so would have been to reject Yahweh for another god and to have turned her back on what it was that made her a people.

Moreover, since religion and politics were inseparable in the unitive world view of the ancient Near East, this meant that Israel's own organization had to maintain the form it had been given when she became Yahweh's people. For this reason she never established herself in one of the city-kingdoms of Palestine, continuing the amphictyonic polity even when she had, in terms of the areas held by the constituent tribes, come to hold considerable territory in Palestine. This is why the independence

of the clans and tribes within the confederation was maintained
with fierce jealousy, Israel as a whole being rallied to united action only by Yahweh himself through charismatic leaders in
times of crisis.[21] This is why the center of the confederation was
neither a permanently located capital nor a city-kingdom with a
temple of the usual kind, but was merely a temporary "resting
place" for Yahweh's sacred palladium, the ark, at which the
tribes could rally and which could be moved when necessary.[22]
It should be stressed again that so dynamic was the conviction
behind all this that it not only worked for two centuries but
prospered. Here, Israel could maintain, is a God who is God
indeed and here a people whose foundations are sure. For evidence she could point not only to her origin and her continued
existence, but to the way in which she had prospered and grown
in a world in which her ways and her faith denied so much that
was taken for granted.

Only against this background can Israel's fate in the late
eleventh century be adequately appreciated for the blow that it
was. The arrival of the Philistines in southwest Palestine, their
consolidation into a powerful pentapolis in which were included
five formerly Canaanite city-kingdoms, and their subsequent determined expansion into the territory dominated by the Israelite
amphictyony presented a threat the like of which Israel had not
before known. The Philistine advance broke up the amphictyony,
reduced its members to the status of subjects of the Philistines,
destroyed its last great central shrine, and enabled the Philistines to take possession of the sacred ark.[23] The Philistine rout
of the amphictyony encouraged neighbors of lesser importance
to strike at Israel too, and it was, apparently, such a move by the
Ammonites against Jabesh in Gilead that resulted in the appearance of Saul to rally the tribes in the manner of a traditional,
charismatic leader.[24] Though the stories of Saul are recounted
in the light of the later presence of monarchy as an institution
in Israel, possibly to assure later Israel that the Judahite house

of David was not solely responsible for bringing kingship to God's people, Saul's rise must be looked upon as the last violent but futile gasp of the vitality of the old order in Israel.[25]

The result, first, of the decisive victory of the Philistines at Ebenezer at which the ark was captured and of the subsequent destruction of Shiloh and, second, of the final Philistine crushing at Mount Gilboa of the last-ditch amphictyonic effort under Saul, was that Israel, to all intents and purposes, no longer existed. Remaining in a Palestine dominated by the Philistines were only the scattered remnants of the old confederation. History had given the lie to the claims made by Israel for her God and for her own destiny under him. Her credo had been unique. She could not, in the fashion of the culture around her, continue to recite it with new divine characters substituted for a defeated Yahweh. Everything was gone. The vague remembrance of the depth of this disaster, of the shattering of Israel's faith and the destruction of the institutions in which that faith had been maintained, is echoed in passing allusions to it in the Old Testament literature.[26]

In order to understand the Israel existing once again when David had finished all that is recounted in II Sam. chaps. 1-6, it is necessary to take into account the radical break described above, and to view the monarchy as no simple continuation of what had preceded it. David did indeed succeed in bringing Israel back into existence, and the amphictyony did find, under him, a new center and the ark a new "resting place."[27] Israel's existence was now, however, only one aspect of the existence of an empire that had its center in the city-kingdom of Jerusalem and included other Canaanite cities as well as Judah and a number of subject peoples. The center of the amphictyony and the "resting place" of the ark was a Near Eastern cult center with its own mythological traditions, with its own originally Canaanite priesthood, and with everything Israel had hitherto eschewed and resisted.[28] All this is recognized in the ambiguous position

of the Old Testament as a whole with regard to just where Israel's
real beginnings lie and where the covenant originated. On the
one hand, the E stratum of the Pentateuch and Deuteronomy
concentrate on the Mosaic covenant at Sinai/Horeb. On the
other hand, the traditions found in II Sam. chap. 7, in many of
the psalms, and by implication in J stress the covenant with
David at Jerusalem. Moreover it is possible for the Chronicler
to write a history of Israel in which nothing at all is made of the
covenant of Sinai/Horeb or of Moses, and in which everything
before David is merely summarized in genealogies.

    This ambiguity was recognized from the beginning of the
kingdom by those whose roots were most firmly located in the
old amphictyony and its traditions. They could not deny that
Israel had come to life anew in the Davidic kingdom and all that
went with it but, for them, the preservation of the traditions of
the amphictyony in the framework of a Near Eastern cult and
mythology of the type resisted for so long by Israel was subversive of the very things David had kept alive. This lay behind the
unrest that even in David's time led to the revolt of Absalom and,
more importantly, to the revolt of Sheba.[29] It was the underlying
cause of the secession of Israel from the Davidic kingdom after
the death of Solomon.[30] Furthermore the ambiguity of seeking
to define Israel in terms of an age and a polity which no longer
existed led to the increasingly reactionary religious spirit producing the tumultuous first century of the northern kingdom and
the violent "prophetic" revolution against the Omriads. That
spirit finds expression in the Old Testament literature in the
Elijah-Elisha legends, E, Deuteronomy, and the deuteronomic
literature in Joshua through II Kings. While this literature provides our chief sources of knowledge for the unique faith of the
old amphictyony, it was in its time reactionary propaganda seeking to solve the tensions and ambiguities of a living present by
groping for a past that was gone.[31]

    It was, however, a fact that the uniqueness of the faith of

the ancient Israelite amphictyony was preserved only in the new thing wrought in the era of David and Solomon. This is why the creative nucleus of the Old Testament was that provided by the J writer, who himself probably came from other than strictly "Israelite" circles in the Jerusalem court. By adopting the unique Israelite credo as his basic point of view because he saw it as a more adequate explanation of reality than the mythical approaches of ancient Near Eastern culture, by relating that credo and its implications to what Israel had inherited by becoming a part of that culture, and by seeing the Davidic achievement as the newest phase in the ongoing purpose of Yahweh in history as well as the fulfillment of all that had preceded it, the J writer made Israel's point of view a live, present option rather than a reactionary refuge. Under the blows of the Philistines the old Israel had died. Yahweh, however, had not died. Of that the new covenant with David, in which the old covenant with Moses was not denied but fulfilled, was the sign.

The statement of the first fact lays the groundwork for the second and third, which may be stated more briefly.

II

The second fact is that the seeds of all later future hope, of all later messianism in the broadest sense of that word, lay in what Israel had experienced historically under David and Solomon. That under Israel's God a glorious future could succeed the collapse of an equally glorious past was, for those who had eyes to see, the meaning of the new, Davidic Israel. Israel's eschatological hope, however varied might be its expressions in centuries to come, rested squarely on the historical fact that in the kingdom of which David and his dynasty were the center and symbol Israel had risen from death to new life. Furthermore, because that resurrection had made the boundaries of Yahweh's rule more inclusive than before by taking in Judah and Jerusalem and many other elements, Israel's authentic eschatological hope had always about it a universal character that prevailed over nationalism and exclusiveness. The origin of that kind of hope is indicated by the very term used to denote it. "Messianism" originated in what Israel had experienced under David, the messiah par excellence.[32]

An inescapable consequence of such a view of the origins of messianism and eschatology in Israel is that all that is unique in her faith cannot be traced exclusively to the premonarchic amphictyony, either historically or theologically. It is true that Israel's insistence that the essential locus of Yahweh's revelatory activity lay in historical events in the remembered past, rather than in pretemporal or extraworldly mythical occurrences reflected in the rhythms of nature, originated in the faith of the amphictyony. It is also true that it was of the essence of that faith that God had created a people from what had been "no people" and that it was that creation, not the mythical creation of the physical cosmos, which was central for theology and anthropology. It is further true that the amphictyony saw in its own historical existence, in its incredible success and persistence through two centuries of life as a cultural outsider in the ancient world, the real evidence of the power and sovereignty of Yahweh. All that, however, was grounded in the empirical continuation and preservation of an order—life under the amphictyonic covenant—begun by Yahweh in the past. It had no basis on which to affirm that Yahweh and his sovereignty transcended the collapse of one order and the rise of another, for it had had no experience to cause it to contemplate this problem. Thus it was easy enough for that faith to have nothing to do with the wider cosmic and mythological speculation of the culture surrounding ancient Israel. This too explains why the sources of our knowledge of the amphictyonic faith—E and Deuteronomy and the northern prophet Hosea—never really explore the implications of Israel's faith for peoples other than Israel.

Only when the old amphictyonic order had collapsed under

the Philistine onslaught and had been supplanted by the new Davidic order could what was unique in the old faith be appropriated and extended in a new way. If the change had come about not because the old faith was untrue but because Yahweh continued to exercise his sovereignty in history, then something more had to be said in which the old faith was not denied but was applied to the newer situation. The J writer did just this. The J epic proclaims how Yahweh—whose essential character had indeed been revealed in the events to which the amphictyonic traditions bore witness—and his purposes transcend even the order in which they had first come to be known and proclaimed. Thus the period of Moses and of amphictyonic life in Palestine can be seen as only one era, albeit a centrally important one, in a purposeful history stretching back through Israel's historical antecedents to the beginning of the world and stretching forward into the Davidic kingdom in which the J writer stands.[33]

Although there is no explicit eschatology in the J epic, its view of the Davidic present as neither discontinuous with nor a denial of the past was, through its affirmation of ongoing history, to become the basis for making further affirmations with regard to new ages and new futures. Only on the basis of the total historical experience of Israel, Davidic as well as amphictyonic, and on the basis of the kind of interpretation given that experience by the J writer, were the prophets from Amos on able so triumphantly to affirm that the sovereign purpose of Yahweh did not collapse with the fall of the Davidic kingdom. For the prophets of the ninth through the seventh centuries lived through a period in which the expansion of the Assyrian and Babylonian empires was bringing the Davidic era to an end, in which Israel as an empirical entity on the stage of history was once again being ground to pieces. Basic in the message of those prophets was not a call to reform, a summons to return to what Israel had been in amphictyonic days or at some other previous point, but the

18 LUX IN LUMINELUX IN LUMINE

belief that precisely the imperial expansion by which Israel was
being swept away was part of the ongoing purpose of Yahweh
and that that purpose was not tied to any one age or polity.[34]
That claim held within itself the implication that whatever age
was being born in the travail through which Israel was passing
in the era of the classical prophets was, as the age born out of
the travail of the Philistine war had been, one in which the purpose of Yahweh discernible in Israel's past would find further
fulfillment. On the basis of this implication voices in the continuing prophetic circles of the exilic and postexilic ages were
able to continue to be affirmative about their tragic present as
well as hopeful for the future. And all this could come about
because of what had been implanted in Israel's faith as a result
of the accomplishment of David and its interpretation by the J
writer. It could come about because of what had been revealed
in the miracle of resurrection that took place when the corpse
of amphictyonic Israel arose to new life in the Davidic kingdom.

Furthermore Israel's eschatological hope, although often
self-centered and self-righteous, usually included in some way
other nations, the Gentiles. From the J writer onward, there
were always those in Israel who recognized that the knowledge
of the true God vouchsafed to her, in which she discerned such
meaning for history and hope for its outcome, was held in trust
and had to do with history as a whole. This kind of outlook in
Israel also took its origin in the way in which J had related Israel's faith and hope to the existence and problem of all mankind in the Davidic age when, through the empire of David, the
destinies of others than the original members of the amphictyony
were being drawn into the orbit of Israel's history. Moreover this
kind of outlook finds its fullest expression in that prophetic tradition most closely connected with Jerusalem and the central elements of Davidic theology, the tradition beginning with Isaiah
and preserved in the book bearing his name. Any attempt to interpret the prophetic witness only in terms of the faith of pre-

monarchic Israel, to see the prophetic message as a recalling of Israel to the past, cannot do justice to all this.[35]

To locate all that is distinctively Israelite in the period before the monarchy is, therefore, historically wrong and theologically inadequate. That had to be proclaimed to Israel by the prophets, Amos, for example, inveighing against the self-righteous legalism of the northern successors of those who had sought to return to the age of Moses in their secession from the house of David and in the so-called prophetic revolution against the house of Omri. So profound was the lesson learned by Israel in the Davidic resurrection of her life as a people that the successors of Isaiah could, in an age so desperate and tumultuous as to produce either sheer hopelessness or blind groping for the past, call Israel to put the glories of the past out of mind in anticipation of "new things" to be wrought by the living God. In the same vein Jeremiah, or more likely a successor of that prophet, could proclaim the coming of a day in which the new action of God would be so glorious as to erase even the exodus from Egypt as the sure evidence of his sovereign power (cf. Isa. 43:18-19; Jer. 23:7). The latter is made the more remarkable by the fact that Jeremiah and the tradition flowing from him are much more prone than Isaiah to point to the Mosaic age as the definitive period of Israel's existence.

Thus did the events in the time of David provide Israel with a characteristic attitude toward changing history and its new futures. All this, of course, is not to deny the complexity of the question of the origins and history of messianism and eschatology in Israel.[36] The cult, mythology, and sacral kingship mediated to Israel through the traditions of Jebusite Jerusalem played their part.[37] So did the desperate plight of the Jews in the postexilic age when earthly hope seemed impossible and the influence of Iranian dualism was felt.[38] And there is much more to it than that. Neither is this to deny that Israel's eschatological imagery was complex and varied. The exodus, Moses, Elijah, creation-resurrection mythology, and many other things than the Davidic messiah figured in the manifold pictures of the eschaton. Still, what has been said up to this point does mean that the primary origins of Israelite eschatology, its possibility, cannot be located either in premonarchic Israel or in something Israel picked up along the line. It means that those origins are to be found in the historical remembrance of the fact that Yahweh had once, in specific historical circumstances, brought his Israel back to life again when she had been dead. Those origins are to be found in the experience of the reconstitution of the old Israel in a new form under David, and in that experience as interpreted for what it was under God by those who neither looked in a reactionary way exclusively to the past nor uncritically swallowed everything that came with being an ancient Near Eastern kingdom.

III

Finally it is a fact, as unavoidable for the theologian as for the historian, that only because Israel's faith came to be related to the culture in which she existed, in terms of all that Jerusalem and the Davidic monarchy brought with them, have we heard of her at all. Admittedly that faith had about it a vitality which enabled the older amphictyonic polity to survive two centuries of settled existence in the midst of ancient Near Eastern culture before the beginning of the monarchy. Furthermore that vitality was such that, when Israel took on the culture, the Israelite monarchy was unique. The fact remains, however, that the formative nucleus of the Old Testament provided by the J writer came into existence only when the success of the Davidic monarchy demanded such an epic account of her origins as was usual in the culture of the time and place. The psalms indicate that behind such an epic lay the thoroughly non-Israelite conception of a recounting of how Israel's God had come to prevail over the other gods, and that Israel was definitely part of her culture.[39] The point is that in the literary and cultic forms of her age, mediated to her in what she appropriated of Canaanite culture, Israel bore the witness to her faith which is preserved for us in the Old Testament. We cannot escape the fact, for example, that the cultic thought world of the Priestly Code which provides the framework of the completed Pentateuch came ultimately, in spite of the later date of that code itself, from pre-Israelite, pagan Jerusalem.

It is true that the recovery, by contemporary scholarship, of the cultural world in which ancient Israel lived has resulted in a new knowledge and appreciation of the uniqueness of Israel's point of view.[40] That knowledge and appreciation, carried down into the age of Jesus and the New Testament, is currently working a revolution in theology. That revolution, however, must not lose sight of what is equally given as the uniqueness of Israel (and the New Testament): the way in which that uniqueness was able continually to relate itself to the culture in which it existed so that the culture became the means by which the faith was proclaimed and passed on. It is theologically irresponsible either to overlook this or simply to record it as a historical but lamentable fact. It is also theologically untrue to the Bible itself. Something theological has to be said about it, something that claims for it a significance under God in terms of his purpose. To do so is to continue in the tradition of the J writer and of the classical prophets who saw the sovereignty of the living God as something operating with the same power in their present as it had in the formative past. To do so, it may also be added, is to continue in the tradition of St. Paul and the great Fathers of the Church's early history who saw that what God had wrought in Jesus Christ was something infinitely greater than could be discussed merely in terms of the issues present within the Jewish community where it had begun.

It should be stated that there is an obvious distinction between claiming theological significance for something and accepting that something as true and not subject to criticism. If both the theology and the anthropology implicit in ancient Near Eastern cultic mythology were fundamentally incompatible with the theology and anthropology implicit in Israel's point of view, that incompatibility could be recognized for what it is while, at the same time, the fact of the significance of that mythology as the vessel in which Israel's faith was preserved and applied to new situations could be recognized for what it is. If, to take another example, the philosophical presuppositions of the Fathers of the Church were fundamentally incompatible with what the Old and New Testaments were saying, that could be recognized without failing to do justice to the fact that the Church confesses Jesus Christ today only because behind it lies a history in which the gospel was wrestled with in terms crucial to the world into which it first came. It can be recognized and, at the same time, the age of the Fathers affirmed as a principal means by which the One whom the Bible proclaims as God can be God for us. To insist that theology speak only in the language of one age or culture or philosophical system is to be obscurantist. It is, however, to be obscurantist in a different way to deny any historical or theological significance to the successive ages and cultures and philosophical systems through which the theological data have been mediated to us. It is also to be untrue to the theologically affirmative attitude toward ongoing history that is basic to biblical faith. For the Bible, since the age of David, has insisted that the process by which the theological data have come to us is itself part of the data.

2

The "Prophet" in
New Testament Christology

BY JOHN KNOX

It is a familiar fact that in the eschatological expectation of ancient Israel the divinely endowed agent or mediator of God's
final judgment and redemption often appeared as an ideal King,
Priest, or Prophet.[1] It has been argued that these three roles
were originally used to designate three different and separate
conceptions of the "Messiah," each characteristic of a different
community or tradition. This appears to be too simple an account. The King is certainly the dominant figure among the
three, and this ideal King must always have had in some degree
both priestly and prophetic functions. Still, the several roles are
distinctive and could be emphasized in various ways to produce
quite different pictures of the Coming One. In certain forms of
the eschatological hope in which no King, or "Messiah" in the
strictest sense of that term, appears (God himself was King and
would bring his rule to pass without intermediary), the Prophet,
who heralded this divine action, could become the supreme eschatological personage. In the Dead Sea Scrolls, not to mention
the earlier-known Damascus Document, we have evidence of a
belief in two "Messiahs," one the King and the other the Priest;
and the Prophet is mentioned in close connection.[2] Sometimes
a particular way of combining the roles was occasioned by the
actual rise of some individual who in certain circles was hailed
as the expected One. If this individual was in fact the High
Priest as well as the King, as in the case of certain Hasmonean
princes, the two roles, and perhaps the Prophet's as well, were

fused by history itself. The supreme instance of this kind of fusion is, of course, the early Church's conviction that all the authentic hopes of Israel, whatever their precise form, were fulfilled in Jesus as the Christ.

This being true, it is at first sight strange that in the New
Testament relatively little emphasis is laid on the category of the
Prophet in the interpretation of Jesus' messianic role. Much is
made of his being the King, the Son of David. Here one thinks
especially, but not alone, of the Synoptic Gospels. One important book of the New Testament, the Epistle to the Hebrews,
is devoted to a presentation of him as the Great High Priest,
and the rest of the canon is not without hints that he was sometimes thought of so. And, needless to say, other later and basi-
cally unmessianic categories were also employed, such as the Son
of Man, the Servant, and the Logos. But relatively little is made
of Jesus as the Great Prophet. Why should this be? One would
have supposed, in advance, that this office would have seemed to
the Church most obviously applicable. Jesus had been not at all
like a priest or a king, but he had actually been a prophet. Had
he not been called such by others and had he not even referred
so to himself? [3]

Oscar Cullmann notes the relative neglect of the category
among early Christians (only among the heretical "Jewish
Christians" did it become important) and accounts for its disuse by its inadequacy in various ways. It was, he says, "too narrow to comprehend the whole fullness of the person and work
of Christ." [4] But could not this be said almost, if not equally,
truly of the other comparable categories? Was any one of the
existing traditional terms adequate? Was it not the insufficiency
of every single category which accounts for the Church's appropriation of *all* the categories, along with whatever fresh terms
it could find? Furthermore it is important to remember that the
Church was able to enlarge and enrich whatever traditional categories it employed—note what it did to the conceptions of Priest

and King—and that it could have transformed the role of the
Prophet as well. Indeed Cullmann finds that the Fourth Gospel
has done precisely that. The prophet's "word" has become the
Logos!

Actually, however, one does not need to invoke some religious or theological inadequacy to explain the relative disuse of
the category in the primitive period. One has only to recall a
simple matter of fact. The very first disciples of Jesus had in all
probability been disciples, just before, of a man whom they had
come firmly and surely to regard as the Prophet; and although
they now had a new master, they were not ready to dispossess
their old one of this role. (The Fourth Gospel does, but this is
much later.) John the Baptist was and, so far as these first Christians were concerned, would continue to be the Prophet, Elijah
redivivus. To Jesus might be ascribed all the other traditional
terms and offices, but that of the Prophet had been already occupied and pre-empted. It belonged, for them at least, irrevoca-
bly to John.

Fully to understand this continuing loyalty to John on the
part of the earliest Christians, it would be necessary to know
much more than we do about the connections both between
Jesus and John and between the two movements they initiated.
There can be no question, however, that these connections were
close indeed. Both the Synoptic Gospels and the Fourth associate
the beginnings of Jesus' public career with John's activity; and
although it is only the Fourth Gospel which actually records
that some of his earliest followers had been disciples of John,
this is so likely in the nature of the case that we can trust the
fact. Besides there are clear hints of it in both the Synoptics and
Acts. John's name appears in the Gospels almost as often as the
names of all the disciples of Jesus combined, and there are constant references by Jesus and others to his significance in connection with Jesus' own work. Indeed it would appear that Jesus
himself had been at one time John's disciple—unquestionably

he was baptized by John—and Matt. 11:7 ff. indicates not only
the high and warm regard Jesus felt for John but also, more specifically, that he too thought of John as the Prophet, the fulfillment of Malachi's prediction of a Prophet-Messiah, and that he
was now looking momentarily for the kingdom of God and the
Son of Man, of whose coming John had been the divinely appointed herald and precursor.

If Jesus had been thus closely related to John and if he regarded John in the way this passage in Matthew plainly indicates, we shall not expect to find any rivalry between them or,
in the beginning, between the communities of their disciples.
It is likely that John had been imprisoned, and perhaps executed,
before Jesus' work began[5]; but, even if not, it is clear that Jesus
was never in any sense a competitor of John. He took up, in his
own characteristic and quite different fashion, the work which
John had been or would soon be forced to lay down. The disciples of John did not reject John—did not need to reject him—
in order to become disciples of Jesus. Having given the messianic
role to John, they were not asked to ascribe it now to Jesus. There
must have been an interval—we shall not even guess how long
—after they became attached to Jesus before they began to think
of him as the Messiah in any sense of that term. In that interval
John could still be thought of so, and there is every reason to
believe he was. If we are to trust Matt. 11:7 ff., Jesus himself
thought of John so—at least in the beginning, perhaps to the
end. In this way, the idea that John was Elijah the Prophet-
Messiah became well established even within the nascent
Church.

What happened when (whether early or late) Jesus came
to be recognized as the Christ was not a displacing of John in
the Prophet's role, but a transformation of the role itself. The
Prophet, who in Malachi was to go before the face of the Lord
(in the sense of Yahweh) and to prepare his way, and was thus
in a real sense the "Messiah" himself, began to be conceived of

as going before the *Messiah's* face and preparing *his* way. John could thus continue to be regarded as the Prophet, even though Jesus had taken his place as the supreme eschatological figure.[6]

I have been speaking of a "relative disuse," and it is important to observe the concession implicit in that term. I have referred to the evidence which Cullmann adduces that among the "Jewish Christians" Jesus was thought of primarily as the Prophet, "the true Prophet." [7] The sources he cites are comparatively late and show us a semi-Gnostic second-century sect; but the origins of this sect may well be primitive and its Christology (or, as Cullmann prefers to put it, its "Prophetology"), equally ancient. Mark 6:14 ff. (and parallels) is enough to put beyond question that, during the latter decades of the first century, there were persons—are they to be called Christians?—who thought of Jesus as Elijah *redivivus* or as "one of the prophets" (which I would understand to mean "whichever of the prophets might be thought of as fulfilling the eschatological expectation of *the* Prophet"). Others apparently, having first identified John the Baptist as the Prophet, had concluded that Jesus was John raised from the dead.[8] In all of this we have undeniable evidence of the existence of a Prophet-Christology as applied to Jesus. But we cannot actually trace this earlier than Mark's Gospel; and in any case it is mentioned only to be decisively repudiated. The whole point of the Synoptists in this connection is not that Jesus is in any sense the Prophet, but that he is *not*. Apparently, for the great majority in the communities for which the Synoptic Gospels (each and all of them) spoke, Jesus was not thought of as Elijah, or as the Prophet under whatever name. I suggest that he was not thought of so, simply because the central Christian movement, which the Synoptists represented, had important roots in the work and continuing influence of John the Baptist and that the particular identity of the eschatological Prophet had been pre-empted by him.

Later we may believe, as the original vivid memory of John

the Baptist receded, the tendency to ascribe all eschatological titles to Jesus alone led to some effort to reclaim this one, too. One sees this rather clearly in the Fourth Gospel, where John's being the Prophet is definitely denied and, possibly, some reinterpreting of the Prophet's role, to make it more suitable to Jesus, is attempted. I should say the same tendency appears also and perhaps somewhat earlier in Acts 7:37 and Acts 3:22-26. But in neither of these passages is the identification of Jesus with the Prophet quite clear and forthright, although it seems to be implied.[9] Cullmann points out that, so far as the canonical sources go, only in the Gospel of John and in the early chapters of Acts does the idea of Jesus as the eschatological Prophet appear.[10] This might be taken as evidence that a primitive conception failed to commend itself. I find it more plausible to explain the appearance of the idea only in Acts and John (both relatively late works) by the Church's later tendency to utilize every possible Christological category to interpret Jesus.[11]

When we limit the appearances of Jesus as the Prophet to early Acts and the Fourth Gospel, we are not disregarding the evidence that, in some quarters at least, he was thought of as analogous to Moses, as being even a "new Moses." That Christians before the end of the first century regarded Jesus as superseding Moses, "fulfilling" him in some way, is true and important. This conception is especially manifest in Matthew (although W. D. Davies thinks its significance there has been exaggerated [12]); and if C. F. Evans is right in his understanding of the central section of Luke as having been based on Deuteronomy,[13] it is almost as important in the third Gospel as in the first. The Prologue of the Fourth Gospel contrasts Moses, through whom was given "the law," with Jesus, through whom came "grace and truth"; and in the sixth chapter of this Gospel the author seems to be setting the new "exodus" in Christ over against the old exodus under Moses, the "bread from heaven" over against the "manna in the wilderness." In Paul, too, anticipatory hints of the same analogy and contrast can be found.

All of this amounts to a massive body of evidence—and there is more.[14] I do not believe it can be used, however, to support the view that any large body of Christians (even in the period of the Gospels) regarded Jesus as the eschatological Prophet who was to be the immediate herald of the kingdom of God and in whose arrival it would first appear. The "new Moses" idea could belong, and apparently often did belong, within a different context of thought. Despite Moses' connection with prophecy and despite Deut. 18:15, 18, where he predicts the coming of a prophet like himself, Moses is never in the New Testament referred to as "prophet," nor, except in the Fourth Gospel (notably John 6:14), is that term used in connection with Jesus' role in leading the "new exodus" or in promulgating the "new Torah." In a word, at least so far as the earlier parts of the New Testament are concerned, the eschatological Prophet is not Moses but Elijah. Moreover not only is John the Baptist clearly identified as such, but the identification is so firmly understood that Jesus is never given that title in the primitive period, and rarely later. The title was reduced to fit John as the Christians now thought of him (the forerunner of the Christ), not maintained in its original high sense and adapted to fit Jesus as the Christ himself.

A quite different view of this primitive phase of Christology is presented in two brilliant articles by J. A. T. Robinson.[15] His argument is intricate and one cannot do justice to it in any summary, but the following notes will indicate its general direction and conclusions: (1) John the Baptist did not think of himself as Elijah but (2) he did picture the Coming One in that role. (3) When Jesus appeared and was acknowledged by John as the Messiah, the latter expected him to fulfill the role of Elijah (hence his doubts and questions during his imprisonment). (4) Jesus was at first accepted as Elijah by his disciples. (5) It was Jesus who first identified John as Elijah, but only slowly was

this identification accepted by others, and never quite completely
(witness the Fourth Gospel's denial). (6) In the very earliest
thought of the Church, Jesus was not the Christ during his
earthly life, or even after the resurrection, but was rather the
"Christ-elect." He was yet to be made the Messiah and to come
as such. Therefore (7) in the earliest Christology, most clearly
reflected in Acts 3:12-26, Jesus could be *both* Prophet *and*
Christ. The human, earthly Jesus was the Prophet-forerunner
of the "Christ he [was] to be." (8) The canticle in Luke 1:68 ff.,
celebrating Elijah *redivivus*, which actually appears in the story
of the birth of John, can and should be recognized as having
been originally composed with Jesus' birth in mind.

I shall make no attempt to present the evidence on which
Bishop Robinson relies at each of these points or to convey the
cumulative effect of his argument as a whole. I shall hope that
the reader of these comments of mine will have read, or will
read, the articles themselves.

I have no difficulty in agreeing that John the Baptist probably did not think of himself as Elijah. I find it harder to decide,
on the basis of the scanty sources, that he was expecting Elijah,
that he at first recognized Jesus as this prophet, and was therefore later disturbed and perplexed when Jesus did not conform
to the Elijah type. Still all of this too may be true. I find myself
also agreeing with Bishop Robinson that in the earliest Christian
confession Jesus was not the Christ during his earthly life, but
was, so to speak, the Christ-elect, although I see no adequate
reason for doubting that it was the resurrection which constituted his exaltation to the Messiah's office. But to go the rest of
the way with Robinson is more difficult. That Jesus during his
human career was regarded as Elijah by any significant number
of his disciples or that this career was later thought of in such
a way seems to me most unlikely. I feel forced to reject this view,
not only because of the absence of sufficient evidence to support
it, whether in the Gospels or elsewhere in the New Testament,

but also because of the difficulty *a priori* in supposing that any messianic role, once held by Jesus, could have been taken from him. According to Bishop Robinson's scheme, Jesus was at first accepted as Elijah. A little later, not only did the Church vigorously deny that he was Elijah, but also just as vigorously affirmed that the Prophet's role had been filled by quite another, namely, John. Finally, the assertion is later being made again (in the Fourth Gospel) that Jesus and no other was the Prophet. Is such a scheme inherently probable? Would any messianic office or function, once assigned to Jesus, have been given by his disciples to another? Surely the actual evidence for such an unlikely development would need to be strong indeed, whereas in this case the evidence is notably weak. Much the stronger argument can be made for the view that insofar as Elijah's, or the Prophet's, role figured at all in early Christian thinking, it was assigned from the beginning to John. The supposition of Bishop Robinson that it was Jesus who first identified John with Elijah may or may not be true. But if true, there is every indication that the identification was at once accepted both by those disciples of John who had become disciples of Jesus and by other disciples of John as well.

This brings us to Bishop Robinson's final point, his claim for the Christian origin of the canticle in Luke 1:68 ff. It has been characteristic of recent study of the early chapters of Luke's Gospel to assign the original composition of this canticle to so-called "Baptists"—that is, to a religious community which stemmed directly from the circle of John the Baptist's followers and which, it is claimed, maintained an independent cult life of some kind for a century or so.[16] Bishop Robinson, much too cavalierly in my opinion, dismisses the evidence for the existence of this community. This evidence is truly enough not copious or massive, but in its measure it is *there,* and it cannot be ignored. Even if it be granted that so far as the second and later centuries are concerned the sources are questionable as well as scant, this cannot be said of the first century, which after all is the only period we are really concerned with at the moment. Acts 18:25 and 19:1-7 put the continuing existence of a "Baptist" community of some kind entirely beyond doubt. The indications that, at this stage in its life at any rate, it stood in a close relation to the Church do not obscure the fact that it was *not* the Church. And if some of its members (such as Apollos and the "disciples" whom Paul baptized at Ephesus) were willing to reconsider John's prophetic role and to accept the Church's assignment to John of a greatly subordinate and merely preparatory function, we can hardly doubt that there were others of them who would not have been so tractable.

Actual evidence of the existence of these more recalcitrant "Baptists" or "Johannists" is furnished by the author of the Fourth Gospel whose references to John simply cannot be otherwise explained. Why should he interrupt the exalted theological argument of the Prologue with negative references to John the Baptist? And how shall we understand his opening the actual narrative of his Gospel with vigorous denials of certain specific roles to John? Robinson answers that "the denials and disclaimers recorded of John . . . (John 1:8,15, 20-23, 30 f.; 3:27-30) are in fact perfectly natural and in accord with the Synoptic tradition (Mark 1:7 f. and pars.; Acts 13:25)." [17] As to the "accord" with the Synoptic teaching, a great deal of ingenuity would be required to harmonize Matt. 11:14 ("He [John] is Elijah who is to come") with John 1:20 ("They asked him [John], 'What then? Are you Elijah?' He said, 'I am not.'"). How "natural" the "denials and disclaimers" are must be a matter of opinion, but I dare say that most critical readers of the first three chapters of the Fourth Gospel will regard them as "natural" only if a polemical purpose can be attributed to them. The important point is not that the writer *thinks* as he does, but that he *speaks* as he does. One might agree that Mark, if asked or challenged, would also have said, in effect at least, that John "was not that light"; but the fact is that Mark does not say so, presumably because he was *not* asked or challenged. Why does the author of the Fourth Gospel say—what occasion would he have had to say—that John was *not* "the Christ" or "Elijah," or "the Prophet" if there were not those in his environment who were saying that he was all three? Robinson describes such an argument as "circular," [18] but this is hardly the case. The signs of polemic in the Fourth Gospel's treatment of John the Baptist would have been noted by critical scholars and the indicated inference drawn from them, even if there had been no other evidence whatever for the existence of a "Johannine" or "Baptist" movement.

"That there were elements of John's following which did not find their way into the Church is indeed very probable," Bishop Robinson writes; "that the elements constituted a rival group to Christianity in the first century, with a competing Christology, is, I believe, without any foundation whatever." [19] This statement is, to me, by no means clear or consistent. It is to be presumed that by the first clause in it more is meant than the obvious fact that some of John's disciples may not have become Christians; Robinson must mean also that they continued to be in some sense John's disciples (surely Apollos and the Ephesian "disciples" did). But if this is true, how could they have avoided having some kind of Christology? And if, by common agreement, it was not the Christology of the Church, how could it have failed to be in some sense "competing"?

If the survival, even if only for a few decades, of a "Baptist" community of any kind should be granted, one is bound to think of it in reading the first two chapters of Luke. Especially because this community was very near to the Church, and with interlocking origins, it is almost inevitable that one should find the ultimate source of some of the materials in these chapters in its cult life. This section of Luke obviously represents the intertwining of two birth narratives—one of Jesus and one of John. In both cases there are angelic annunciations; in both, miraculous con-

ceptions; in both, the circumcision and the naming (in accord-
ance with angelic instructions) on the eighth day; in both,
canticles of praise at the birth of a Saviour. No one will doubt for
a moment that Luke regards all of this material as belonging ap-
propriately to the Church and as redounding to the honor and
praise of Jesus as the Christ. There is no difficulty in understanding how the Church could adapt and absorb the Johannine material it found in its possession. The significant question is
whether the Church could, or would, have created it in the first
place.[20]

In this connection Bishop Robinson's argument takes an
unusual turn. He does not deny that the canticle Luke 1:68 ff.
celebrates the birth of the "Messiah"—that is, the supreme eschatological person—albeit under the form of Elijah, *the* Prophet;
and he agrees that it is inconceivable the canticle should have
originated elsewhere than in a community which believed that
this Prophet-Messiah had come. But he denies that this community was thinking of John. *Jesus* was not only the Christ to be
but also and even then Elijah, and this hymn, written originally
to celebrate *his* birth (not John's), had its first setting in a *Christian* community. In taking this position, however, Robinson
lays himself open to what may appear to be a fatal objection:
How, in that case, could a *Christian* evangelist ever have used it
in connection with *John's* birth? That the Church could have
come to regard a canticle actually celebrating John's messiahship
(in the loose sense of that term) as being really intended to celebrate that of Jesus is surely far more easily credible than that it
should have taken a canticle originally expressing its own adora-
tion of Jesus as the Prophet-Christ and applied it to John.[21] The
whole tendency in the tradition, not least apparent in Luke-Acts,
toward a progressive depreciation of John, as Jesus' significance
was more and more fully realized, runs counter to such a development.

3

Pistis Iēsou Christou

BY E. V. N. GOETCHIUS

When Paul first proclaimed what we now refer to as his doctrine of justification by faith, some people accepted it with joy and others rejected it in horror, though not all of those who accepted or rejected it seem to have understood it in the same way.[1] Similarly mixed feelings have prevailed in regard to this celebrated doctrine down to the present day, together with similarly various ways of understanding what Paul meant.[2]

It is easy to understand how this confused state of affairs arose and why it is so difficult to escape, for Paul's statements of the doctrine all involve a combination of ambiguities. We shall merely mention the difficulty of understanding exactly what Paul meant by *dikaioō* and related forms[3] and pass at once to the basic problem; for whatever Paul meant by "justification," it is plain that in his view the only sort worth having cannot be had apart from what he calls *pistis Iēsou Christou*.[4] It is to the interpretation of this expression that this essay is devoted.

The expression *pistis Iēsou Christou* is difficult to interpret because it is doubly ambiguous: it is lexically ambiguous because *pistis* has more than one "dictionary" meaning, and it is grammatically ambiguous because the genitive case can indicate more than one kind of relationship.[5]

The meanings of *pistis* are divided by many writers into active and passive:[6] the active meanings are given in English by such words as "faith," "trust," "confidence," and "belief," while the passive ones are indicated by "faithfulness," "fidelity," "trustworthiness," "loyalty," and "reliability." The "links which con-

nect the two extremes, the passive with the active meaning," are
given by J. B. Lightfoot as "fidelity, constancy, reliance, trust,
belief" [7]—a sequence which at least suggests the semantic range
of *pistis,* apart from a few somewhat technical senses such as
"oath," "proof," and "pledge." [8]

Scholars are generally agreed that *pistis,* in the New Testament, sometimes has "active" meanings, sometimes "passive."
Thus *pistis* is usually or often translated by "faithfulness" in Matt.
23:23,[9] Rom. 3:3,[10] Gal. 5:22,[11] and Tit. 2:10,[12] and by "faith"
in Jas. 2:14, 17, 18, 20, 22, etc.[13] There is, indeed, very broad
agreement that *pistis* should be understood as "faith" (= belief)
in the expression *pistis Iēsou Christou,*[14] but here and there voices
are raised in favor of "faithfulness" (= trustworthiness),[15] and a
few writers try to straddle the issue and understand both meanings at the same time.[16]

The lexical meaning of *pistis* in Rom. 3:22, 26, Gal. 2:16,
and similar passages cannot be determined apart from the question of the grammatical meaning of the genitive case of *Iēsou
Christou* and its synonyms. Contrariwise, the relationship expressed by the Greek genitive is not a precise one,[17] and cannot
be determined exactly apart from the lexical meanings of the
words involved and the context in which they occur. A brief
examination of a few English examples will make it easier to
understand the complex nature of the relationship between lexical and grammatical meanings.

Superficially, the four expressions "John's car," "John's arrival," "John's capture," and "John's kindness" have the same
grammatical structure, yet the relationship indicated by the
English possessive morpheme *'s* is not the same for all four.
"John's car" conveys more or less the same information as "John
has a car"; "John's arrival" is equivalent in the same way to "John
arrived" (or "John is arriving" or "John will arrive," etc.); "John's
capture" implies either that John captured someone (or something) or that someone (or something) captured John (= John

was captured); and, finally, "John's kindness" implies much the
same thing as "John is kind." [18] It will be seen at once that each
of the four expressions we began with implies an expression
which has a grammatical structure quite different from that of
the expression implied by any other one, and it is also apparent
that the form of the implied expression depends on the nature of
the noun (other than "John") in the original expression. In the
remainder of this essay expressions which imply one another
in this way will be called "transforms" of each other.[19] Further,
nouns which behave like "car" [20] (e.g., wife, house, typewriter,
book, etc.) will be described as "object-nouns"; nouns which
behave like "arrival" [21] (e.g., departure, death, appearance, jour-
ney, etc.) will be called "intransitive event-nouns"; nouns which
behave like "capture" [22] (e.g., arrest, embarrassment, etc.) will
be called "active" or "passive event-nouns" according as the
transforms associated with them are of the form "(John) captured (someone)" or "(someone) captured (John)," respectively;[23] finally, nouns which behave like "kindness" [24] (e.g.,
modesty, humility, goodness, truth, etc.) will be called "ab-
stracts."

By proceeding in this way we may divide all English nouns
into three principal semantic classes (grouping the various types
of event-nouns together) and, conversely, if we know the semantic class of a noun z, we can infer the grammatical meaning
of the expression "John's z." It is along such lines as these that
we actually proceed—less formally, to be sure—when we infer
the meanings of new words from their contexts. For example, if
we encounter the phrase "John's flembor," we can infer only that
"flembor" is a noun;[25] if, however, we read further that "John
has a flembor," we will know that "flembor" is an object-noun
(like "arbor"). Similarly, "John flembored" will tell us that
"flembor" is an event-noun (like "labor"), and "John was flem-
borable" will indicate that "flembor" is an abstract (like
"honor").

Unfortunately, some nouns fit into more than one of these semantic classes; for example, the expression "the love of God" may imply "God loves someone," "someone loves God," "God is loving" (with "loving" understood as a predicate adjective), and possibly even "God has love," so that "love" may be described as an event-word, an abstract or, less probably, an object-word.

When we turn our attention from English to Greek and, particularly, to the expression *pistis Iēsou Christou*, we find immediately that *pistis*, like "love," can belong to more than one semantic class. Thus, for example, forms of the expression *pistin echein* occur twice in the Pauline corpus[26] (Rom. 14:22, I Cor. 13:2), but never with *Iēsous Christos* as subject. We infer, therefore, that *pistis* may sometimes be used by Paul as an object-word, but that he does not so use it in the phrase *pistis Iēsou Christou*, so that here, at least, the relationship indicated by the genitive is not that of possessor to possessed.[27]

The verb most obviously related to *pistis* is, of course, *pisteuein*,[28] which occurs in several expressions that may possibly be regarded as transforms of the expression *pistis Iēsou Christou*. Two of these may conveniently be considered together:

(1) Rom. 9:33; 11:2 (< Isa. 28:16), **ho pisteuōn ep' autōi ou kataischunthēsetai**. The expression in heavy type is itself a (participial) transform of the ("kernel"[29]) form *pisteuei ep' autōi*. The context shows that *autōi* refers to Jesus Christ.

(2) Gal. 2:16, *hēmeis eis Christon Iēsoun episteusamen*, etc.; cf. Rom. 10:14, *pōs oun epikalesōntai* **eis hon ouk episteusan**. The expression in heavy type from Rom. 10:14 is a relative (and negative) transform of *pisteuei eis (auton)*; from the context it appears again that the pronoun refers to Jesus Christ. Cf. also Phil. 1:29, . . . *to eis auton pisteuein*, which is an infinitive transform from a similar "kernel" form.

Are we justified in regarding either or both of the expressions (1) *pisteuei*[30] *epi Iēsou Christōi* and (2) *pisteuei eis Iēsoun Christon* as a transform or transforms underlying the expression *pistis Iēsou Christou?* If so, the translation of Gal. 2:16b must be something like that given by most English versions, i.e., *We have believed in Christ Jesus in order that we may be justified by faith in Christ.* This may be correct, but it has a tautological ring, so that the contextual proximity of the hypothetically related expressions may indicate some kind of contrast rather than synonymy. In view of this, further investigation is necessary. In the first place, it is obvious that *pisteuei eis Iēsoun Christon* may very properly be understood as a transform of *hē pistis autou [hē] eis Iēsoun Christon,* and an expression similar to the latter actually occurs in Col. 2:5, . . . *tēs eis Christon pisteōs humōn.* Can we regard this expression as semantically equivalent to *hē pistis Iēsou Christou* except for the presence of the genitive pronoun? If so, *hē pistis Iēsou Christou* must be exactly equivalent to *hē pistis eis Iēsoun Christon.*[31] This last expression fairly obviously means "the *pistis* which is directed toward Jesus Christ," so that we could proceed to infer that the genitive in *pistis Iēsou Christou* is objective. A similar inference could be drawn from the kernel form (1) *pisteuei epi tōi Iēsou Christōi,* especially since no expression of the form *hē pistis epi tōi Iēsou Christōi* occurs.[32] Against this conclusion, which is accepted by most scholars, it may be urged that neither (1) nor (2) exactly fits the requirements of a transform for *pistis Iēsou Christou* and that we should, therefore, look further.

A third construction of interest to us is *pisteuō tini ti,* in which the verb has the meaning "entrust" (cf. John 2:24). *Iēsous Christos* does not occur in the Pauline epistles as the subject of *pisteuō tini ti,* but it is possible to understand that Jesus Christ is the unnamed "performer of the action" in certain passages in which this construction occurs in the passive voice. Thus Gal. 2:7, *pepisteumai to euaggelion,* and I Cor. 9:17, *oikonomian pepisteumai,* may be regarded as passive transforms of (*Iēsous Christos*) *pepisteuken moi to euaggelion* and (*Iēsous Christos*) *pepisteuken moi oikonomian,* respectively, although the phrase *hupo tou theou* in I Thess. 2:4 (*dedokimasmetha hupo tou theou pisteuthēnai to euaggelion*) seems to indicate that Paul thought of God, rather than Christ, as the "performer of the action" here.[33] However, if Jesus Christ *is* understood as the performer of the action in these expressions, they may possibly be regarded as transforms of *pistis Iēsou Christou,* which would then have to be rendered in English as "the trust of [i.e., given by] Jesus Christ," or "Jesus Christ's trust" (*sc.* of the gospel, etc., to us). *Pistis* can, in fact, have the meaning "trust" (= that which is entrusted),[34] but there is insufficient evidence to support this interpretation here.[35]

The verb *pisteuō* occurs in several other constructions, but for the present we may ignore most of them, since in the Pauline corpus *Iēsous Christos* does not occur in them as either subject or object. So far as the Pauline epistles are concerned, therefore, an examination of these constructions will provide us with no further direct evidence for regarding *pistis* (in *pistis Iēsou Christou*) as an event-noun.

We have next to ask whether *pistis* (in *pistis Iēsou Christou*) may be an abstract. If it is, we should expect to find expressions in which Jesus Christ is described by an adjective with the meaning, "having the quality of *pistis.*" An adjective which appears to have this meaning is *pistos,* and this occurs in II Thess. 3:3, *pistos de estin ho kurios.* Since it is clear from the context that *ho kurios* here refers to Christ rather than to God,[36] we have a suitable transform for *pistis Iēsou Christou.* The adjective *pistos* corresponds to English "faithful" and has both of its senses: (1) trustworthy, worthy of faith, worthy to be trusted, and (2) trusting, full of faith, believing.[37] If the second meaning were correct here we would expect to find equivalent expressions of the form *Iēsous Christos pisteuei* (with *pisteuō* used absolutely or followed by a simple dative, *epi* + dative or accusative, *eis* + accusative, or possibly by a simple accusative or by some other prepositional phrase) but, as we have already seen, such expressions do not occur. Thus *pistos* should be understood with this second meaning in Gal. 3:9, . . . *sun tōi pistōi Abraam,* since the expression *Abraam episteusen tōi theōi* also occurs (Rom. 4:3, Gal. 3:6; both from Gen. 15:6), but in *pistos ho kurios* the first meaning must be understood. Hence *pistos ho kurios* means "the Lord is trustworthy," and *pistis Iēsou Christou,* regarded as a transform of this, must mean "the trustworthiness of Jesus Christ."

The evidence that we have examined is meager, and our examination of it has led us to conflicting conclusions. If we are to make further progress we shall obviously have to enlarge the scope of our investigation. We shall do this by comparing *pistis Iēsou Christou* and its possible transforms with other expressions which are similar in form.

For the expression *pistis Iēsou Christou* (which we shall for convenience refer to as (A1)) we find parallels:

(A2) Rom. 3:3, *hē pistis tou theou*[38]

(A3) Rom. 4:16, *pistis Abraam* (cf. Rom. 4:12)

(A4) Phil. 1:27, *hē pistis tou euaggeliou*[39]

These four expressions, all of which have the pattern *pistis* + genitive, will be called expressions of type A.

For the expression (B1) *hē pistis eis* (or *pros*) *Christon* (cf. Philemon, verse 5; Col. 2:5) we find a parallel:

(B2) *hē pistis eis* (or *pros*) *theon* (cf. I Thess. 1:8).

However, no parallels of the form (B3) *hē pistis eis* (or *pros*) *Abraam* or (B4) *hē pistis eis* (or *pros*) + N[40] occur in the Pauline epistles. Expressions which have the pattern *pistis* + preposition + noun will be called expressions of type B.

For the expression (C1) *pistos ho kurios* (cf. II Thess. 3:3) we have parallels:

(C2) *pistos ho theos* (I Cor. 1:9; 10:13; II Cor. 1:18; I Thess. 5:24)

(C3) *pistos Abraam* (Gal. 3:9)

(C4) *pistos ho logos* (cf. I Tim. 1:15)

Expressions which have the pattern *pistos* + noun (where the noun is in the same case) will be called expressions of type C.

For the expression (D1) *pistos tōi Christōi* (cf. Acts 16:15;

cf. also Eph. 1:1 *pistos en Christōi*) we have a parallel in:

(D2) *pistos eis theon* (I Pet. 1:21)

However, expressions of the form (D3) *pistos* + *Abraam* (dative) or + preposition + *Abraam* or (D4) *pistos* + N (in the dative) or + preposition + N [41] do not occur. Expressions which have the pattern *pistos* + noun (dative) or + preposition + noun will be called expressions of type D.

It will be seen at once that *pistis* and *pistos* exhibit similar syntactic behavior; however, when we come to *pisteuō*, the patterns are different. Here we find:

(E1) *pisteuei tōi Christōi* (cf. John 5:38, etc.)

pisteuei epi tōi Christōi (cf. Rom. 9:33)

pisteuei epi ton Christon (cf. Acts 9:42)

pisteuei eis ton Christon (cf. Gal. 2:16)

To these there are obvious parallels in:

(E2) *pisteuei tōi theōi* (cf. Rom. 4:3; Gal. 3:6)

pisteuei epi tōi theōi (cf. Acts 11:17 D)

pisteuei epi ton theon (cf. Rom. 4:5, 24)

pisteuei eis ton theon (cf. John 12:44b, etc.)

No parallels of the form (E3) *pisteuei tōi Abraam* (or *pisteuei epi* or *eis Abraam*) occur, but we do find parallels of the form:

(E4) *pisteuei tēi akoēi hēmōn* (cf. Rom. 10:16)

pisteuei epi pasin . . . (cf. Luke 24:25)

pisteuei eis to onoma (cf. John 1:12, etc.)

Expressions which have patterns of the form *pisteuei* + dative or + preposition + noun will be called expressions of type E.

Finally, there are no expressions in which *Christos* (or one of its synonyms), *theos*, or a noun (of the sort which occur in A4, C4, and E4) occurs as the subject of *pisteuei*,[42] but we do have:

(F3) *Abraam episteusen tōi theōi* (cf. Rom. 4:3, Gal. 3:6),

which we may call expressions of type F.

It may now be seen, from an examination of the parallel expressions assembled above, that the nouns which occur with *pistis, pistos,* and *pisteuei* (in the place of the noun in the patterns described above) may be divided into three groups. The first group includes *Christos, theos,* and their synonyms; the second includes *Abraam* and, presumably, other nouns denoting persons; and the third group includes all other nouns. Nouns of the first group can occur in expressions of types A, B, C, D, and E; nouns of the second group can occur in expressions of types A, C, and F; and nouns of the third group can occur in expressions of types A, C, and E.

The unique expression of type F provides the key to the interpretation of the rest. This expression can only mean "Abraham believes (trusts, has faith in) God," so that if expressions (A3) and (C3) are understood as transforms of this, they must be rendered in such a way as to show that faith (belief, trust, etc.) proceeds from Abraham. In the case of (C3) this can be done only by translating "faithful (i.e., trusting, believing) Abraham," but in the case of (A3) it may be done in two ways, by translating "the faith (trust, belief) of Abraham (*sc.* in God)" or, to make the relationship to (C3) clear, by translating "the faithfulness (or fidelity) of Abraham (*sc.* toward God)."

Similarly, expressions of the form (E4) must mean something like "(someone) believes (in) the gospel, the report, the word," etc., so that if (A4) and (C4) are to be understood as transforms of (E4), they must be rendered in such a way as to show that the "belief," "trust," "faith," etc., is to be directed toward "the gospel," "the truth," etc. Again, this can be done for (C4) in only one way, namely, by translating as "the word is trustworthy (= worthy to receive belief)." For (A4), on the other hand, the translation may be done in two ways, first by translating as "faith (belief, trust) in the gospel, word," etc., and second, to show the relationship to (C4), by translating as "the trustworthiness of the gospel," etc.

The analysis of the remaining expressions is more complicated. Let us begin with expressions of the form (E2), which evi-

dently mean something like "(someone) believes (in) God." If
(A2), (B2), (C2), and (D2) are to be understood as transforms
of (E2), they must be rendered in such a way as to show that the
"belief," "trust," "faith," etc., is to be directed "toward God." In
the case of (C2) this may be done by translating as "God is trustworthy" (cf. (C4)), whereas for (D2) it may be done by translating as "faithful to (or, trusting in) God" (cf. (C3)). Thus
pistos may have either its active sense (believing, trusting, having
faith) or its passive sense (worthy of belief, trustworthy) when it
is connected with *theos*, depending on the way in which the
connection is made. This leads us to expect similar semantic behavior from *pistis* in view of its similar syntax. Thus in translating
(B2) we can preserve the idea that "faith," "belief," "trust," etc.,
is to be directed "toward God" simply by rendering "faith (belief,
trust) in God" or, equally well, by rendering "faithfulness (fidelity) toward God." The latter translation serves to show the relationship to (D2), and this suggests that a similar relationship
exists between (C2) and (A2). That is, (A2) is to be understood as semantically distinct from (B2) just as (C2) is semantically distinct from (D2), and in the same way; accordingly,
(A2) is to be translated as "the trustworthiness of God." [43]

Since it is clear that the syntactic parallelism between (A1),
(B1), (C1), (D1), and (E1), on the one hand, and (A2), (B2),
(C2), (D2), and (E2), on the other, is quite exact, the former
expressions should be translated like the latter, namely, as:

    (A1) the trustworthiness of Christ
    (B1) faith in Christ *or* faithfulness toward Christ
    (C1) Christ is trustworthy
    (D1) faithful to (trusting in) Christ
    (E1) (someone) believes (in) Christ

Of these interpretations only (A1) is seriously contested, but no
other interpretation appears to fit the over-all syntactic and semantic pattern of Paul's style so well.

The arguments presented in this essay are intended to be

illustrative of syntactic and semantic analytic procedure; they cannot, of course, be regarded as conclusive. Even if they were elaborated to take account of other semantic and syntactic relationships, their cogency is necessarily limited by the small size of the Pauline corpus. Linguistic analyses of the sort attempted here will always have to be supplemented by analyses on other levels; such a "higher" level of analysis might, for example, take the form of a comparison of the various metaphors which, like "justification by faith," Paul uses to describe God's saving action. Theologically "loaded" expressions like "justification by faith" are difficult to handle by any methods. It would be very advantageous if studies could be made of the syntactic and semantic behavior of a number of theologically neutral terms and metaphors, for such studies could serve as valuable guides and controls for the investigation of terms and metaphors with theological overtones. Without such neutral guides and controls there is always the danger that theological considerations will prejudice the result of an investigation before all the relevant philological considerations have been given their proper weight.

4

The Image of God and the Prosopic Union in Nestorius' *Bazaar of Heracleides*

BY ROWAN A. GREER III

The Christological definition formulated at Chalcedon in 451 was designed to resolve a controversy which had begun a quarter-century earlier in Constantinople. Nestorius, the patriarch, began his tenure of office by attacking the custom of calling the Virgin *Theotokos* or "Bearer of God." His sermons against this title set off a doctrinal battle which resulted in his exile and the eventual defeat of the Antiochene school of which he was representative. The Antiochene Christology had been developed in an explicitly anti-Apollinarian way by Diodore of Tarsus and received its most careful and sophisticated expression at the hands of Diodore's pupil, Theodore of Mopsuestia. Nestorius' Christology, in turn, can be understood only in terms of the position defined by Theodore.

The characteristic feature of the Antiochene Christology was its refusal to predicate the human attributes of Christ to the divine nature and its tendency to speak of the subject of those attributes as "the Man." There were a number of factors which led the Antiochenes to posit a double predication with regard to Christ's person. In the first place, their insistence upon God's immutability and impassibility required that no change or passion could be ascribed to the Word, even indirectly. Second, their notion of grace and free will involved them in arguing that man's freedom to respond to God's grace must be maintained. In order for Christ to be human he must possess a human will; and this

46

implied a human subject in Christ's person. Third, the Apollinarian denial of the full humanity of Christ led to an Antiochene reaction which strongly emphasized that humanity.

The fundamental problem of the Alexandrian Christology, represented by Cyril, was how to express adequately Christ's humanity. On the other hand, the fundamental difficulty faced by the Antiochenes concerned formulating the union between the two subjects of attribution they were led to posit. The Antiochenes actually parceled out scriptural texts to "the assuming Word" and "the assumed Man." How were the two one Christ? Theodore's most careful answer to the question states the union in terms of the Word's indwelling the Man by good pleasure "as in [a] Son." He attempts to solve the problem by employing the biblical categories of indwelling, good pleasure, and sonship. The solution is less a strictly metaphysical one than a metaphorical and even poetic one. Certainly none of the technical categories of the eclectic Platonism of his time appear centrally in Theodore's definition. Nevertheless, his thought reflects those categories; and in certain passages he attempts to use the word *prosōpon* as a term descriptive of the Christological union. Theodore, however, nowhere in his extant writings develops this aspect of his thought.

In contrast, although Nestorius' Christology does not abandon the biblical foundation laid by Theodore, it does begin with the *prosōpon* speculation. His definition of the union states that the *prosōpon* of the Word and the *prosōpon* of the Man are joined in one *prosōpon* of union. He opposes this formula to Cyril's doctrine that the two natures of the divinity and the humanity are united in one hypostasis of the Incarnate Word. Nestorius' argument depends in part upon denying that a nature or essence can exist without hypostatic expression. Both the human nature and the divine nature must have their own hypostases. *Prosōpon*, on the other hand, refers to the outward expression of an essence or nature, and the one outward expression of Christ's

prosōpon can still be analyzed into two distinct hypostases as
well as two distinct natures and essences.

In what follows we shall not be primarily interested in the
more strictly philosophical aspects of the prosopic union. Indeed,
we should suggest that they are precisely what makes Nestorius'
apology, *The Bazaar of Heracleides,* so obscure a work. The
terminological battle has the effect of making it difficult to see
what Nestorius is driving at. On the contrary, our concern will be
with the biblical and metaphorical categories Nestorius uses to
propound his prosopic union and fill it with meaning. The Antiochene Christology, as it appears in the *Bazaar,* is closely and carefully expounded in terms of a fully developed technical vocabulary, including such words as *phusis* and *prosōpon.* But Nestorius'
real contribution lies in his ability to go far beyond the limits
of such a vocabulary. This is possible largely through his use of
the biblical doctrine of the image of God. By stating the doctrine
of the prosopic union in terms, first, of Phil., chapter 2, and,
second, of the *imago Dei,* Nestorius is able by a kind of theological alchemy to transform the barren categories of what might
otherwise be a stultified philosophy into something very much
alive.

One of the principal ways in which Nestorius explains his
doctrine of prosopic union is by referring to the passage from
Phil., chapter 2, in which Christ is described as one "Who, being
in the form of God, thought it not robbery to be equal with God;
but made himself of no reputation, and took upon him the form
of a servant." A typical example of Nestorius' exegesis of this
passage follows:

> For this reason the Apostle lays down the *prosōpon* of the un-
> ion and next the things wherefrom the union results. He says first
> *the likeness of God,* which is the similitude of God and next *it took
> the likeness of a servant,* not the *ousia* nor the nature but the *schēma*
> and the *prosōpon,* in order that he might participate in the likeness
> of a servant, and that the likeness of the servant might participate

in the likeness of God, so that of necessity there might be one *prosōpon* from the two natures. For the likeness is the *prosōpon,* so that it is the one by *ousia* and the other by union in respect to the humiliation and to the exaltation.[1]

The passage from Philippians speaks of "the form of a servant" and also of the exaltation of the servant and the giving of the "name above every name" to Jesus. That name is, of course, "Lord"; and the title implies that Jesus is somehow identified with the Lord of the Old Testament, the God of Israel. Regardless of the original meaning of the passage, Nestorius sees in it an expression in more vivid terms of what he has called prosopic union. The "form of the servant" is the *prosōpon* of the humanity; the "form of God" is the *prosōpon* of the divinity. And in Christ these two *prosōpa* become one *prosōpon.* The form of God humbly takes the *prosōpon* of the servant; the form of the servant is exalted to become the *prosōpon* of God. This takes place without any change or confusion of the *ousia* or the nature of either the humanity or the divinity. While it is self-evident that St. Paul did not intend to teach the doctrine of prosopic union, it is nonetheless clear that the imagery of Phil., chapter 2, goes very far toward helping Nestorius to explain the purport of the prosopic union.

In Nestorius' view Phil., chapter 2, implies another idea. Even in the passage cited above, the use of the word "likeness" may be noted. Remember that God is said to have created man in his own "image and likeness." Phil., chapter 2, manages to convey the meaning of the prosopic union; but a certain amount of precision is necessary before Nestorius can really be said to have made himself understood. That precision is achieved through the use of the doctrine of the image of God. In other words, Nestorius uses Gen. 1:26-27 to explain Phil., chapter 2. The resulting exegesis expounds not only the text but also the prosopic union. And it involves a great many ideas which have no explicit expression in either Genesis or Philippians, for example

the Adam typology as explaining the redemption wrought in
Christ. All of this is less confusing in fact than it is in analysis;
therefore, let us examine a passage from the *Bazaar*:

> This in fact is the chief greatness of the nature of humanity:
> that, since he remains in the nature of humanity, he accepts *a name
> which is more excellent than all names*; neither in consequence of
> moral progress nor in consequence of knowledge and faith, but
> therein by virtue of his readiness to accept [it] has it come about
> that it should become his *eikon* and his *prosōpon* in such wise that
> his *prosōpon* is also the *prosōpon* of the other. And he is both God
> and man, and the likeness of God in condescension and in *kenosis*
> and in *schēma*, [and] the likeness of the flesh as man; and the man
> is by exaltation what God is, through the name which is above all
> names.[2]

The prosopic union, as illustrated by Phil., chapter 2, is here
understood in terms of the creation and redemption of man in
the image of God. The words *prosōpon* and "image" are used as
equivalents. Nestorius could hardly have hit upon a more adequate way of expressing the prosopic union. The perfection of
human nature can be described as the "image of God." Man was
created in that image, and Christ is the second Adam and the
visible expression of the image of God inasmuch as he is perfect
man. Thus the image of God can be thought of as the *prosōpon* of
the humanity. On the other hand, the image of God can be understood as the perfect expression *ad modum recipientis* of who God
is. That is to say, God must reveal himself in terms that can be
understood by his creatures. Since we are men, we must understand him in human terms, and his expression of himself comes
to us in that way. Therefore the image of God is the perfect expression of God to us men. The image of God, understood in
this sense, can be thought of as the divine *prosōpon*. God dwells
in Christ and perfectly reveals himself to men through him. Yet
the two *prosōpa* are really one because both the humanity and the
divinity are the image of God.

From one point of view there is adequate precedent in the patristic tradition for Nestorius' understanding. The orthodox Logos theology, stemming in part from Origen's synthesis, understood the Logos to be the image of God. However, Nestorius' insistence upon the human image of God in Christ's person, together with his reassertion of the strictly biblical foundation of the doctrine, marks his position as strikingly original. Furthermore the metaphor has the advantage of avoiding any confusion of the two natures or the two *ousiai*, because, while the *prosōpon* of union is directly related to the two realities, there is no substantial union of the two. As Nestorius says:

> As God appeared and spoke unto Adam in *schēma*, and as it was none other, so will God be [seen] of all men in the natural *schēma* which has been created, that is, that of the flesh, appearing and speaking in his own image and the image in the Archetype. So that on the one hand God appeared in the image, since he is not visible, on the other hand the image is conceived as representing him who appeared not. For it is not [the fact] that the image is his being, but that on the other hand the very image and *prosōpon* [are] the humanity of the divinity and the divinity of the humanity.[3]

Nestorius' doctrine does not involve the same kind of substantial union envisaged by the hypostatic union. Rather the union between the humanity and the divinity in Christ is the community and perfect union between God and man that was intended at creation, when man was created by God in his image. By using this series of ideas, Nestorius has managed to reassert the fundamental Antiochene position, and has succeeded in divorcing his prosopic union from confusion with the hypostatic union.

The line of reasoning that has just been adduced may be pursued somewhat further. First, let us examine the way in which Nestorius describes God's activity in recreating the image of God in Christ. The prosopic union, understood in terms of the image of God, certainly involves first of all God's own expression of himself in the union. And it is this expression that is equivalent to the recreation of the image, and the whole work of redemption from the Godward side:

> . . . for, because God created the first man in his own image and in his likeness and the *prosōpa* of God the Maker—of the Father and of the Son and of the Holy Spirit,—were not revealed to us, so that we might also know the Creator and obtain completely the teaching of the Divine knowledge and receive in completeness a complete idea of the image of God, he has renewed all creation in Christ and has made known and shown unto us what the Maker is.[4]

Christ is the perfect revelation of God, of the creator to the creation. It is this revelation that draws all mankind to the "knowledge of God." This knowledge is a moral and spiritual knowledge, and not simply an intellectual one. It is the knowledge that gives us perfect communion with God himself, and enables us to become in fact what we are by intention and promise, *viz.*, the image of God. Here in Nestorius' thought is no suggestion of a substantial union whereby men can be divinized and brought into the Godhead. Rather God's activity in the prosopic union is thought of largely in terms of the fulfillment of what was begun at creation, and redemption as the completion of the creation rather than its eradication by divinization.

The next step in our reasoning must be to show what man's part in the *imago Dei* is. It is perfectly natural that Nestorius should devote more attention to this aspect of the prosopic union, for it will be remembered that his critique of the Alexandrian view centers upon the loss of the humanity in the hypostasis of union. Nestorius does not lose sight of the fact that God is the one who fashions the image of God in Christ. That is, redemption is before all else the work and gift of God. This work, however, must involve man's free cooperation as well:

> But this was also so for his own sake; because of his unlimited obedience [it was] that he died for sinners. Both in his will and in

his thought he acquired, in short, naught else than to wish and to will whatsoever God willed in him. For this reason God also was in him whatsoever he was himself, in such wise that he also became in God whatsoever God was in him for the forming of his coming into being in his likeness, [to wit] the *prosōpon* of God. . . .[5]

God forms Christ in his own image, but this formation is possible only because Christ exercises his free will as a man in obedience to God's will. Perhaps the most moving aspect of the Antiochene theology is the way in which there is conveyed a sense that Christ's battle is a type of our own, and his life so deeply an ensample for us, that we can see ourselves in him. The moral and spiritual meaning of the doctrine that Christ is *homoousios* with us finds expression as follows:

. . . for until the time of his victory he was striving to make firm in God the image which had been given unto him. But because he stablished his own image in all temptations perfectly and without failing and without falling short in anything, he comported himself on our behalf, being zealous to rescue us captives from the violence of the tyrant and to draw us towards him and to make all of us the sons of his own kingdom, the associates and the heirs and the sons of God.[6]

Christ is, indeed, the "captain of our salvation." By affirming in his humanity the perfection of man, the image of God, he shows us how we must fight our own battle.

The affirmation that Christ is man in the same sense that we are men is made even clearer by the way Nestorius handles the Adam typology. Christ was not simply created in the image of God and sent to us as such; he was a man like Adam, and the possibility of sin was open to him:

Because in fact he took this [likeness] in order to abolish the guilt of the first man and in order to give to his nature the former image which he had lost through his guilt, rightly he took that which had proved itself guilty and had been made captive and had been subjected to servitude, with all the bonds of scorn and contempt.[7]

The nature that sinned is the nature in which the Word chose
to dwell. This indwelling depended first upon God's choice of
the man Jesus, but also upon the man's obedience and response
to the indwelling Word. What "had rendered itself guilty" in
Adam, in Christ is made perfectly obedient, so that the image of
God is truly established.

Nestorius goes on to explain what he means, in the passage
just cited, by using the example of a son and heir. When he is
still young, the child cannot come into possession of his heritage.
Rather he must school himself for that possession by a period of
obedience to his father. So Christ comes into possession of his
heritage (the image of God) only at the end of a period of
obedience. This implies something that is perhaps more explicit
in the writings of Theodore: that the perfection of the union
of the assumed Man and the assuming Word, and the perfection
of the image of God, comes only at the resurrection, when Christ
has remained obedient unto death. The entire Christology of
the Antiochenes is by this notion cast not so much in the mold
of timeless concepts as it is in terms of the whole story of
Christ's life of obedience. This is done so that it may be perfectly clear that the human nature was subject to the same human
conditions that limit our lives. In Nestorius' words, the Word
took the nature which had sinned ". . . lest in taking a nature
which was not subject unto sins he should be supposed not to
have sinned on account of the nature and not on account of his
obedience." [8] Adam completed the image of the devil by his
disobedience; Christ completed the image of God, intended by
God for Adam, by his obedience. The Adam typology is in much
the same form here as it is in Irenaeus' writings. In fact Nestorius'
use of the typology is very much like Irenaeus' notion of the
anakephalaiosis. But emphasis is put not only upon God's grace
and choice but also upon the part of the human will in the scheme
of things.

Discussion of the Adam typology and the image of God raises the question of how Nestorius views the image of God apart from his Christology. The answer seems to be that he really does not discuss the image of God save in close conjunction with his Christology. In Irenaeus and the majority of patristic writers, the doctrine of the image of God and the Adam typology are discussed at great length. The nature of man and the question of whether or not man retains the image but not the likeness of God after the Fall, or neither—all this furnishes matter for much discussion. But in the *Bazaar* the preoccupation is so largely Christological that Nestorius almost never discusses the image of God in itself. This produces the interesting effect of focusing attention not so much upon man's creation in the image of God as upon the image of God in Christ. It is understood that man disobeyed God and that the Fall took place somehow. But it is not clear whether this was a falling away from a state of righteousness or the falling short of an innocent nature. This does not interest Nestorius so much as the fact of the image of God in Christ. On the one hand, Nestorius' use of the doctrine does tend to tie his Christology to the more general scheme of creation, the nature of man, and redemption. On the other hand, the preoccupation of the *Bazaar* with the Christological question means that the doctrine of the *imago Dei* is given a narrower application and expression than one might expect. This phenomenon is largely attributable to the fact that Nestorius is engaged in polemic rather than in systematic theology; and it is hardly fair to pass adverse judgment on him on the basis of the meager evidence extant.

Before the digression of the last paragraph, it was stated that Nestorius uses the Adam typology to point out the voluntary nature of Christ's attainment of the image of God. Not only does the human nature have a part in effecting the image of God, but the obedience of the human nature, proceeding from the

exercise of free will, is absolutely necessary for the establishment
of the union between the two natures. In other words, the prosopic union is dependent both upon God's action and upon man's
free will:

> . . . it was preferable to him that the will of God should be
> done and not that of the flesh; and in actions he made himself a
> likeness to will that which he wills, that there might be one and
> the same will in both of them, and one *prosōpon* without divi-
> sion. . . .
> For [to have] the *prosōpon* of God is to will what God wills,
> whose *prosōpon* he has.[9]

It could hardly be more evident that the prosopic union is what
might be called a voluntarist as opposed to a substantial union.

Because many scholars tend to dismiss the Antiochene theology abruptly, simply by saying that the Christological union is
for it simply a voluntary or moral one, something must be said
with regard to such a verdict. We have reached the fundamental
watershed between Alexandria and Antioch. It is perfectly true
that if one confines one's viewpoint to the Alexandrian standard,
a voluntarist union such as Nestorius envisages is hardly an adequate solution. Because the Alexandrian soteriology demanded a
substantial union of God and man, Cyril believed that the Antiochene solution left no real union between God and man. Hence
there arose the charge that Nestorius separated the natures. The
charge was made to stick because the Alexandrian point of view
was largely in accord with the eclectic, Platonic network of ideas
prevalent at the time. But the Antiochene notion of salvation
and of man's nature was opposed to the Alexandrian. Salvation
meant the fulfillment of the fellowship between God and man
which was the original intention of the creator. Nor could salvation be described so as to obliterate the distinction between
creator and created.

Once the opposition of Antioch and Alexandria be understood, the motivation for and the background of the Antiochene

voluntarist union can be seen. If one can divorce oneself from the Platonic categories in which much patristic thought, even Antiochene, is expressed, then one can begin to see the voluntarist union of Nestorius as a profoundly effective statement of Christ's person. Nestorius' union has to do not so much with the substance or essence of man as with the very roots of man's being as a moral, reasoning creature. Certainly man's dignity derives in part from his freedom and the free exercise of his will. And it is precisely this aspect of the matter that the Alexandrian Christology tends to neglect.

The voluntarist character of Nestorius' Christology is extended to his notion of how redemption wrought in Christ is bestowed upon all men. It is worthwhile to note how this is so:

> Therefore after the victory and after the bringing to nought of death Christ has remained [sharing] in the [same] state of life— a state of life which was brought to nought in Christ—in order that those who are in Christ might comport themselves after the likeness of Christ, not only by the grace of the Resurrection but also by the works and manner of life of each one of them; for the former is universal but the latter individual.[10]

This way of understanding what it was that was done in Christ preserves not only the free will of each individual Christian but also closely reflects our own experience of life. That is, the glorious redemption wrought for us is clearly only partially fulfilled in our present lives. A scheme of things which recognizes the exercise of free will over the period of time requisite for a human life is understandably nearer our experience than one which defines things in concepts that are essentially unrelated to time and space in that they are attempts to analyze being itself. To be sure, the Antiochene way of describing reality is far from the only way. It must simply be pointed out that in respect of describing the moral life, the Antiochene system seems far more relevant than the Alexandrian. Finally it must be noted that despite this emphasis upon human moral autonomy, the nexus of

ideas we have been discussing is firmly placed within the context
of God's providential grace. For Nestorius, as for Theodore, that
grace is primary.

To summarize briefly the conclusions reached thus far, it
has been submitted that Nestorius in his exegesis of Phil., chapter 2, and elsewhere equates the *prosōpon* of union with the
image of God. The image of God is, first, the perfect revelation
ad modum recipientis of God and, second, the perfection of human nature. Thus the same term includes both the human and
the divine *prosōpa*. In the discussion of this, it should be evident
that it was necessary to move from the concept of the *prosōpon*
as the image of God to a consideration of the activity of each
nature participating in that *prosōpon* and in the union. There is,
as well, a movement in Nestorius' thought, from the timeless,
narrowly metaphysical categories of the prosopic union to the
description of that union in terms of God's providential economy
and the human obedience exercised throughout his earthly life
by our Lord. It should be reasonably clear from the citations from
the *Bazaar* that the concept of the image of God serves to explain
and clarify what Nestorius means by the prosopic union. Two
questions remain before we can make some general conclusions
from all of this. The first is: What other images does Nestorius
use to substantiate and expound his doctrine?

To answer this first question, Nestorius does indeed use
other metaphors to explain the prosopic union. He speaks of the
indwelling Word, a figure of speech which conjures up the
whole framework of Theodore's Christology. In a few passages
Nestorius describes the union in the image of the burning bush.[11]
The fire and the bush are one, and yet the two are distinguishable. Another metaphor used by both Nestorius and Theodore
is that of the human nature as the temple in which God dwells.[12]
It is interesting to note that Nestorius rejects the image of the
union of body and soul as a type of the prosopic union. The
union of body and soul is, according to Nestorius, an example

of the union of incomplete natures; whereas the union of God and man in Christ is an example of the union of complete natures. One final illustration that Nestorius uses deserves more extensive comment. In several places he describes the prosopic union in terms of a king who takes the form of a servant:

> As a king and a lord, who has taken the *prosōpon* of a servant as his own *prosōpon* and gives his *prosōpon* to the servant and makes known that he is the other and the other he, is content to be abased in the *prosōpon* of the servant while the servant is revered in the *prosōpon* of the lord and king, and for this reason, even though I should not have said the one for the other nor the other for the one, it is so with both of them who are one and possess the same *prosōpon* —[so] are these things in regard to the two natures which are distinct in *ousia* but are united by love and in the same *prosōpon*.[13]

Actually this illustration is nothing more than a variant of the passage in Phil., chapter 2. And, in making that passage more explicit by a definite example of humiliation and exaltation, the illustration serves to confuse the issue somewhat. The trouble is that there are still two people, the soldier or servant and the king, even though they exchange costumes. Moreover there is still more difficulty if the illustration is thought of as a king taking the form of a servant, because in that case there is really no servant. This is a misleading exposition of the passage in Philippians, whereas the use of the doctrine of the image of God is a thoroughly convincing way of demonstrating the truth of Phil., chapter 2, and the prosopic union. The conclusion must be that the most important, as well as the most frequent, illustration or metaphor used by Nestorius in describing the prosopic union is that of the image of God.

The second question that has been posed is: Does Nestorius provide an adequate statement of the union of the two natures? The question can be answered either from an unsympathetic and Alexandrian point of view or from an Antiochene point of view. It has been submitted that there is a fundamental distinction

between the two, and it can be further argued that neither school
can be considered more "orthodox" than the other, although it is
clear that the balance of tradition tends to follow the Alexandrian. If one adopts the line followed by Cyril, one must as-
suredly reject the prosopic union as totally insufficient. If one
chooses to be sympathetic to the Antiochene school, the answer
is not nearly so simple. Of course, to a great extent the verdict
given is a matter of opinion and depends upon the weight attached to the motivation for the respective formulas. On balance, I should submit that the prosopic union per se does not
provide a formula adequate for stating the union of the two
natures. However, by expanding his doctrine in terms of the
image of God, Nestorius has managed to reassert the fundamental Antiochene position in a moving and impressive way.
One may not be convinced by his terminology, but the illustration carries its own weight and rescues Nestorius' prosopic union from the realm of sophistry. By expounding the Antiochene
Christology in his prosopic union, Nestorius enters Alexandrian
lists. By going on to describe that doctrine in the light of the
image of God, he is reasserting the intention of Theodore's
Christology and distinguishing his position from that of Cyril.

   Yet Nestorius' use of the image of God separates him from
both Theodore and Cyril. And it is in this use that the real contribution of Nestorius to Christology may be found. The *imago
Dei* solves in a fairly coherent way the fundamental problem
of the Antiochene Christology by showing in what sense the
two *prosōpa* of the natures are one *prosōpon*. Furthermore it ties
Nestorius' doctrine to the Bible and to the whole point of view
represented in Scripture. By thinking of the image of God in
terms of Christ's life and the providential activity of God through
that life, Nestorius gives his doctrine the dimension of time and
space and ties it closely to our own human experience. Finally,
even though this must be said with some qualification, the
"image-of-God" aspect of Nestorius' Christology brings that part

of his theology into some relationship with the whole framework of creation and redemption and, to some extent, removes it from the narrow arena of conflict. It must remain true that no human terms can adequately convey the reality of God and of his dispensation toward us. Nevertheless two things can be said of Nestorius' attempt to describe the mystery. First, the prosopic union as a formula is inadequate and confusing. This is so because the terms involved depend upon the Platonic and Stoic nexus of ideas more compatible with the Alexandrian doctrine. Thus the prosopic union, so far as terms alone go, represents a kind of selling out to the Alexandrians. One is left with the feeling that it is not worthwhile imposing a few questionable changes upon the well-established Alexandrian scheme. Second, if anything can rescue Nestorius' doctrine from the objections that have been raised, it is his use of the image of God to expound his Christology. In these terms Nestorius is successful. That success is not in the realm of water-tight philosophical categorization but rather in the realm of conveying in an extremely forceful way the truth that "God was in Christ" and that Christ is one with us.

5

Toward a Contemporary Interpretation
of the Chalcedonian *Definition*

BY R. A. NORRIS, JR.

Of the classical documents of Christian orthodoxy, none has
been subjected to more extensive criticism by contemporary Protestant theologians than the *Definition* of the Council of Chalcedon. In itself this fact is no cause for astonishment. What is
surprising, however, is the degree of general unanimity which
this criticism has achieved in spite of the fact that it stems from
thinkers of widely differing points of view. The common line
taken by a majority of writers can be summarized in two judg-
ments, one positive and the other negative. On the one hand,
the Fathers of the Council are praised for their reaffirmation of
the basic elements of a Christian confession of Jesus as divine
Lord. On the other hand, it is suggested that the intellectual
framework of their statement is inadequate, that the philosophical and theological terminology of the *Definition* has certain
radical drawbacks.[1] Its technical language—so the argument
tends to run—assumes a way of understanding God and man
which is probably inconsistent with the outlook of the Scriptures,
and in any case is incapable of giving a positive or self-consistent
account of the Christ of Christian faith. Consequently, if one is
to accept the Chalcedonian *Definition* as a true confession of
Christ, it can only be in spite of what Paul Tillich has called
"the conceptual frame" [2] of its teaching. Many influential theological writers would thus be prepared to agree essentially with
William Temple's well-known youthful judgment that the *Definition* marked "the bankruptcy of Greek patristic theology," [3]
"the definite failure of all attempts to explain the Incarna-

tion in terms of Essence, Substance, Nature, and the like." [4]

But one has only to note this criticism of the *Definition* to recognize that it presupposes answers to a number of important historical and theological questions. Among these questions one looms with special prominence. What exactly is meant by the "theology" or the "conceptual frame" of the Chalcedonian *Definition*? When used in this way, these expressions imply clearly that the Fathers of the Council did in fact either set forth or obviously presuppose a philosophical explanation or interpretation of the Person of Christ which one might compare with, say, the Christological proposals of Bishop Charles Gore. But is this true? And if it is true, then what theory is it that the Fathers set forth or presuppose?

It will hardly do to observe, in answer to this query, that their language is "Greek" or "Platonist." For one thing, these two words tend in contemporary theology to have more a damning than a descriptive function, and one must therefore distrust them. For another, these designations, though no doubt apt enough if they are taken descriptively, tell no more about a fifth-century theological document than the label "scholastic" would tell about a similar document from the fourteenth century. They function, in fact, as little more than an indication of relative date. Further still, this rather summary way of dealing with the question evades the issue of the purpose for which the Fathers employed their "Platonist" language in this instance, and therefore of the *way* in which they used it. Only by settling this issue first can one arrive at a reasonable criticism or appreciation of the Chalcedonian *Definition* in modern terms.

I propose therefore to make a suggestion about one way in which the language of the Chalcedonian *Definition* may legitimately be taken, and therefore about the sense in which the document may be said to have a "theology" or "conceptual frame." On the basis of this suggestion, I shall indicate what seems to me to be a reasonable way of understanding and criticizing the *Definition* from the point of view of contemporary theology.

I

To begin with, however, it is necessary to clarify one or two assumptions on which the argument of this paper is based. The first and most obvious of these is that the language of the *Definition* can be understood properly only in the light of its use in the controversies which provide the historical background of the Council of Chalcedon. It would hardly be necessary to make this point if it were not for the fact that it immediately calls attention to an important consideration which must be kept in mind in any attempt to interpret the *Definition*. The language, that is to say, the technical terminology, of the Council's confession had no one set of agreed meanings. Words like "nature" (*phusis*), "substance" (*hupostasis*), "person" (*prosōpon*), and "essence" (*ousia*) had been used in different ways by various participants in the controversies preceding the Council. Consequently it would have been possible for more than one interpretation of the theological sense of the *Definition* to be given at the time of its composition. The exiled Nestorius was apparently able to make inoffensive sense of Chalcedonian language in the light of his own understanding of its terminology; but this was not the understanding which emerged either from Western reading of the document or from the neo-Chalcedonian Christology of Leontius of Byzantium in the East. Even in its immediate historical context, the *Definition* was susceptible of alternative interpretations, all of which must be accepted as historically (if not theologically) legitimate.

In the second place, it is also true that the Fathers of the Council took their description of Christ as one "substance" in two distinct but inseparable "natures" to be a repetition of the orthodox teaching of early conciliar creeds as this had been expounded against Nestorius by Cyril of Alexandria.[5] Here are two points to be noted. The Council agreed with Cyril in maintaining that the substance and form of an orthodox belief about Christ were at least implicitly contained in the Nicene and Constantinopolitan creeds.[6] Further they acknowledged that in making the terms of this belief more explicit, they were reiterating the position which Cyril had taken against Nestorius. They made their conviction on this point plain by canonizing two letters of Cyril; and they accepted the *Tome* of Pope Leo in the belief that the Roman bishop's anti-Eutychian polemic was in full accord with the teaching of Cyril.[7] The majority of the Fathers of the Council evidently believed that the Christological position which Cyril had adopted in his assault on Nestorius was in all essentials the correct one, and that it excluded not merely Nestorianism, but also the overenthusiastic and misunderstood "Cyrillianism" of Eutyches and Dioscorus. In spite, therefore, of the variety of possible interpretations to which the Council's technical language was open, it seems natural to seek the key to its meaning in the Christology of Cyril.

But—in the third place—this conclusion is no sooner reached than it must be severely qualified, and this on two obvious grounds. For one thing, it is obvious that there are many themes in Cyril's Christological teaching which are in themselves irrelevant to an understanding of the conciliar *Definition* as it stands. The Council Fathers did not seek to supply solutions for all the individual problems which had arisen in the course of the Christological controversies; so inevitably there are great tracts of Cyril's recorded opinions which, whether acceptable to the majority of the Fathers or not, had no direct bearing on the content of their *ekthesis*. The Council was immediately concerned only with the problem of affirming clearly the duality of "elements" within the unity of Christ's Person.

But further still—and more important—there were certain favorite expressions or ideas of Cyril's which the Council was compelled tacitly to repudiate in the light of the Eutychian affair. The phrase "one nature" was dropped,[8] though its Cyrillian equivalent "one substance" was retained. For Cyril's—and the Formula of Reunion's—phrase "out of two natures" the Council (not without debate) substituted the papally sponsored formula "in two natures," [9] doubtless in order to avoid the suggestion that the Incarnation amounts to some sort of fusion of manhood and Deity. Thus the "Cyrillianism" of the Council is a somewhat battered and qualified affair.

Nevertheless—and here we return to our earlier contention —it is perfectly real. The participants in the Council maintained, and modern scholars would on the whole agree with their judgment, that they had preserved and indeed positively reaffirmed the essential substance of Cyril's teaching. If they made or allowed changes in his Christological terminology, this reflected not a repudiation of his position, but an acknowledgment of ambiguities and imprecisions in his language. We might say that their loyalty to Cyril was firm but limited—limited to what they took to be the essential kernel of his teaching.

If then we raise here a question about the meaning of the Council's technical terminology, it is logical to suppose that the critical clue for our answer may be sought in the ideas of Cyril of Alexandria, to whom, after the Councils of Nicaea and Constantinople, the Fathers of Chalcedon made their primary appeal. Nevertheless what we must look for in Cyril is not the precise original of the *Definition* but the way of thinking and talking about the Incarnation which made the Chalcedonian nature-substance terminology *intelligible* to those who adopted it and canonized it. In a way what we shall be asking in the first instance is how Cyril himself used this terminology, or rather, in what frame of reference his usage becomes comprehensible. Then perhaps it will be possible to see in what way and to what extent the logic of his position is embodied in the conciliar *ekthesis,* and what it suggests about the "conceptual frame" of the *Definition* itself.

II

Cyril's purpose in his Christological writings is to assert, as against Nestorius, the unity of Christ as the divine Son who himself has wrought the salvation of mankind.[10] To indicate what is involved in such a confession of the unity of Christ, Cyril employs a number of related expressions. Thus he asserts that Christ is "one nature" or "one substance." [11] At the same time—and presumably as a slightly different way of saying the same thing—he avers that there has taken place in Christ a "natural" or "substantial" union of two different natures or elements, the Word and the flesh, or Godhead and (complete) manhood. In this way Christ is, in his phrase, "one out of both," "one nature after the union." [12]

Now it must be admitted that this language, if taken at face value, is not merely confusing,[13] but suggestive of a number of dangerous possibilities. No one in Cyril's time could help remembering that the expression "one nature" had been the warcry of Apollinaris of Laodicea. And this fact, taken together with what seemed to be the natural force of Cyril's language,[14] brought forth the inevitable charge that he regarded the Incarnation as a quasi-physical mixture in which Deity and humanity are so fused into a single "thing" that neither can survive in its essential character. Was it not necessary to think that Cyril was denying either the full and authentic humanity of Christ or the reality of his Godhead? The Antiochenes whom Nestorius represented had themselves always spoken of a union of two "things" in Christ. But at the same time they had been careful to avoid any suggestion that the two were united in a relationship which presupposed or effected the abolition of their distinction as *two* substances, abidingly different in their unity. Nestorius therefore asked how it was possible to talk of making one thing out of two without at the same time admitting either that the original constituents had their natures modified—violated!—in the result or that one of them was incomplete.

Cyril answers this question—whose force he undoubtedly felt—in two different ways. The first of these, whose characteristic arguments are present in all of his Christological writings, is distinguished by the fact that it tacitly accepts the hypothesis on the basis of which the question posed by his opponents was asked. That is to say, it accepts the presupposition—common both to the Antiochene "Word-man" and the Alexandrian "Word-flesh" traditions in Christology—that the unity of Christ's person is to be conceived as the product of some sort of putting together of two "things," Deity and manhood. In this strain Cyril replies to his critics that the conclusions which they try to force from his Christological formulas are both unintended and unnecessary. They are unintended because he does not *mean* to deny the fullness of Christ's manhood, or to assert a kind of metamorphosis of the divine Son, or to suggest that in Christ the two natures are "confused." They are not necessary because there are ways of combining or putting together two "natures" into one which do not involve the destruction or modification or confusion of the original constituents. As an example of such a union Cyril instances the classical analogy for a "Word-flesh" Christology: that of the union of soul and body to make a man.[15]

But this sort of defense, which became the less convincing as the meaning of admitting a human soul in Christ became clearer, is paralleled in Cyril's writings by another, which is perhaps more distinctively Cyrillian, and which involves a rather different use of terms like "nature" and "substance" for the reason that it works (tacitly) with a different Christological model. In the last resort it is this second form of argument to which Cyril explicitly or implicitly recurs in order to make the meaning of his position intelligible; and it is therefore to this form of his argument that we must attend here.

We may begin by noticing that in both his second and third epistles to Nestorius, Cyril bases the statement of his own position on the language of the creed of the Council of Nicaea—a procedure which the councils of Ephesus and of Chalcedon were to follow. Plainly he understands his own Christological formula to be a development and expansion of what was laid down by the authors of the Church's confession against Arius. But in what particular way? What is it that he seizes upon in this creed?

In his third epistle to Nestorius, Cyril quotes the entire text

Isaiah 7:14

NAME	ADDRESS		PHONE	
OTHER MEMBERS OF FAMILY		BIRTH	BAPTIZED	CONFIRMED

CORRECTIONS   Rector or Parish Office fills out above. Spaces below for Canvasser

POSSIBLE CANDIDATES FOR

BAPTISM

CONFIRMATION

CHURCH SCHOOL

MEN'S CLUB

WOMAN'S AUXILIARY

OTHER ORGANIZATIONS

CONFIDENTIAL REMARKS FOR THE RECTOR (Use other side if necessary)

DATE   SIGNED   CANVASSER of the creed, and paraphrases it thus: "We say that the only-begotten Word of God himself . . . came down for the sake of our salvation, and having lowered himself to the point of self-emptying, was incarnate and made man." [16] This language, he proceeds, lends no credence to the false notion that in the Incarnation there was a transformation of Deity into manhood, or vice versa. But it also rules out any idea that in Christ Deity and manhood are two separate "things" which stand to each other in some sort of external relation. What it says is that there is "one sole Christ, who is the Word (born) of God the Father, together with the flesh which belongs to him." [17] Here Cyril focuses on a different aspect of the Word-flesh scheme. The Incarnation, he says, does not mean a mere conjunction of some sort between the divine Word and a man, as the Antiochenes had traditionally maintained. More important still, the unity of Christ is not the product of any sort of relation or combination of two natures or "things." It consists rather in the fact that it was the one divine Word who took upon himself a new status or form of existence as man. Christ is one because he simply *is* the Word, but now submitting to the limiting forms of a genuine human existence. To speak of Christ is thus to speak of the "one *incarnate* nature [or "substance"] of the Word." [18]

A close examination of this train of thought makes fairly clear what Cyril is trying to say. His theological protest had been called forth by Nestorius' typically Antiochene distaste for the assertion that the divine Word is *properly* called the son of Mary. In thus denying to Mary the style "Mother of God," Nestorius was calling attention to the necessity (as he saw it) of distinguishing two subjects of attribution in the Word incarnate: the Word himself, and the man whom he indwelt. Since it is logically improper either to attribute human characteristics to the Word or to attribute divine characteristics to a human nature, one had to admit that there are in Christ two natures or substances, the Word and the Man, each of which is the distinct subject of his appropriate attributes.

But Cyril would have none of this; and he finds the justification for his attitude in the creed of the Council of Nicaea. For
in that document, as Cyril in effect points out, there is only one
subject of all that is said about Jesus; and that subject is the
Word himself.[19] The human attributes of Christ—his birth of
Mary, his suffering, his death, resurrection, and ascension—are
all, without exception, predicated of the Word. They are not
predicated of a divine-human compound; nor are they predicated
of two natures operating as it were in tandem. Hence, Cyril argues, if the Nicene Creed is a true confession, if the form of
its language about Christ is correct, then there is and can be
only one subject in the Word incarnate. Or, in Cyril's terminology, there is one "substance" of the incarnate Son: the divine
Word himself.

But this, in turn, means something about the humanity of
Christ. It assumes the character of an acquired status, a second
concrete form of existence, which belongs to the Word. To express this idea, Cyril uses the language of "appropriation" which
he had learned in his close study of Athanasius. Manhood is
"appropriated" by the Word in such a way that it may properly
be said to *belong to* him. It becomes as it were a native medium
of his existence and activity. The man Jesus is thus not something else beside the Word of God. He *is* the Word of God
taken in his concrete humanity; and to speak of the "union" of
two natures in Christ is to refer to the process by which the
Word makes a particular human existence his own.

What we must note in this argument is the light which it
sheds on Cyril's use of "substance" (and also of "nature" in those
contexts where he uses it as a functional synonym of "substance"). The word is not given the kind of systematic "philosophical" definition which Nestorius later attempted to give it
in his *Bazaar of Heracleides*.[20] Taken abstractly, it functions as
a shorthand way of referring to the "real subject" of statements
about Christ. In other words, it specifies the general form of an
answer to the question "Who?" as that is asked in connection

with the sayings and doings of Christ. Concretely, therefore, it refers to the Word who, Cyril says, *is* the subject to whom these sayings and doings are properly attributed. Hence to speak of "substantial" or "natural" union does not in the last resort mean, for Cyril, the product of a "putting together" of two contrary but co-equal substances. For him there is unity of substance in Christ in the sense that the Word is one substance, i.e., one subject, which has assumed, appropriated, or entered upon human existence.[21] He explains what he means by "substantial union" in his *Apology against Theodoret*:

> Since therefore Nestorius altogether denies the fleshly birth of the divine Logos, since he introduces [the notion of] a unity which consists in honor alone, and since he says that to God there has been joined a man who is worshiped by reason of his sharing in divine Sonship,—it is inevitable that in struggling against his party we should say that a *substantial union* has taken place. [But] by this expression we intimate nothing save simply that the nature—or substance—of the Logos (that is, the Logos himself), truly united to a human nature without any change or fusion . . . is conceived to be and really is one Christ.[22]

We are drawn therefore to the interesting conclusion that what, in the first instance, governs Cyril's distinctive understanding of the formula "one substance" (and therefore the formula "one nature") is not a physical or metaphysical definition of either term but a perception of what he takes to be the normative grammatical (and logical) form of statements about Christ. The problem to which the formula "one substance" supplies an answer is the problem of how many "subjects" there are in Christ; and the solution itself is based formally on a conclusion drawn from the logical shape of confessional sentences which deal with the Word incarnate.

But this conclusion further offers us a key to Cyril's difficulties with the problem of the two elements or natures in Christ. In this connection, his language is both confused and confusing; and this is not merely because of his habit of using "nature" to

denote alternately both the one subject and the two elements in
Christ. The more basic confusion arises, as we have already suggested, out of the persistence in his thought of the notion that
the two natures are the *things out of which* the one Christ is
made. Cyril's emphasis is always laid on the unity of Christ; and
this fact, together with his inherited habit of speaking of "Word"
and "flesh" as the constituents of the incarnate Son, lead him
instinctively to the use of such expressions as "out of two, one"
and "after the union, one nature." These locutions, however,
have two disadvantages, which Cyril himself perceived only
dimly.

(1) They suggest that the "one substance" or subject in
Christ is a composite of some sort *resulting from* the Incarnation[23]; whereas Cyril himself, as we have seen, understood the
unity of substance not as the product of a "putting together"
but as the immediate reflection of the fact that the divine Word
is the single subject of all that is said of Christ. (2) They suggest
—as the Antiochenes pointed out quickly enough—that the distinction between divinity and humanity in Christ is lost as the
result of their being fused into one. Cyril, as we have seen, never
tires of saying that this is not his meaning. But his protests carried little conviction in the face of the apparent force of his
language.

Nevertheless the protests were perfectly sincere; and Cyril
attempted to convey his real meaning by arguing that while there
is a distinction of natures in Christ which is perfectly real, it is
a distinction which is apparent *only to the mind.*[24] What he
seems to mean by this can be expressed in two propositions. (1)
There are not two "things" or subjects in Christ, but only one.[25]
(2) Nevertheless there are two complete but logically different
systems of predicates which are properly ascribed to the incarnate Word: those which are suited to his status as Word, and
those which are suited to his (acquired) status as man. To grasp
the notional distinction between these sets of predicates is to
"distinguish the natures." But there are not two Christs.

This way of thinking does not mean to deny either the reality of Christ's humanity or the difference between his humanity and his divinity. Its distinctive note lies in the way in which, as a matter of fact, it gets at what is meant by the "natures" in Christ. These are forms of the Word's existence—forms which, in statements about Christ, are defined by the words which compose the logical predicate of a sentence of which the divine Word is the sole logical subject. And the distinction of natures is grasped in the existence of some sort of systematic incompatibility between two classes of attributes which can properly be ascribed to the Word. It is this way of thinking which underlies and renders intelligible Cyril's talk of the union of two elements or natures in Christ.

We can sum this argument up by saying that Cyril took the Word-flesh Christology which he had inherited from Athanasius and Apollinaris, and tacitly reduced it to a subject-attribute Christology whose shape is governed in the last resort by an apprehension of the logical form of traditional statements about the incarnate Word. Underlying, though not replacing, Cyril's use of such images as those of self-emptying, appropriation, and the union of natures is his conviction that to talk about Christ is to talk about the divine Word as exercising a human existence, to speak of one subject in terms which befit both Godhead and manhood. And it is in terms of this Christological grammar that one must in the last resort understand his use of the terms "substance" and "nature."

III

When we return to the Council of Chalcedon from this excursion into the thought of Cyril, it is impossible not to notice that the intelligibility of the decree depends in the last resort upon the subject-attribute scheme which had been Cyril's basic weapon against Nestorius. It is by the retention of this scheme that the Council justifies its claim to be reiterating the essential teaching of the Patriarch of Alexandria.

To say this is not to forget or to deny the modifications
which the Council made in Cyril's language—modifications to
which we have already drawn attention. Neither is it to deny the
debt of the Council to Leo's *Tome* or to the Antiochene "Formula of Reunion." [26] It does however imply that the significance
of these modifications must be estimated in the light of two facts.
First, it should be plain enough (as it seemed plain to the Fathers of the Council) that the doctrine of Christ's existence *in*
two natures could be given a clear and acceptable sense in terms
of Cyril's own Christological language. But second, and perhaps
more important, the Council reaffirmed in no uncertain terms
the basic principle of Cyril's Christology—the idea, that is to
say, of the unicity of "subject" in Christ; and this principle ultimately excludes not merely the Nestorian doctrine of two *hu-
postases,* but also the idea, which had been prominent in Alexandrian circles, that the one substance of Christ is a composite.

Thus the Council begins, like Cyril, by appealing to the
creeds of Nicaea and Constantinople and by affirming their suf-
ficiency in principle as rules of Christological orthodoxy. It notes,
however, that since the promulgation of these creeds, there have
arisen in the Church heresies with which these confessions did
not explicitly deal; and it therefore admits—reluctantly, and contrary to the earlier decision of the Council of Ephesus—the necessity for a new exposition of the tradition in the light of Nestorian and Eutychian errors. With Cyril, then, the Council asserts that in defining its own position, it is doing nothing more.
than "following . . . the holy Fathers"—setting forth the Christological implications of earlier, orthodox confessions.

When at length the Council turns to the statement of its
positive teaching, it begins with an elaborate assertion of the
unity of Christ—Cyril's theme against Nestorius. The nature of
this unity is then explained by the identification of Christ as the
one divine Word, who was begotten of the Father before the
ages, but in the last days was born of Mary for the salvation of
mankind. Thus the one Christ whom the Council confesses is

the divine Son himself—but taken in his dual status as completely divine and completely human. Here the similarity with Cyril's exposition in his epistles against Nestorius is unmistakable. The creeds of Nicaea and Constantinople are understood to affirm—not in so many words, but *by the form of their language*—that there is in Christ only one "thing" and that this "thing" is precisely the eternal Son of God.

As against the Monophysites, it is further said of the incarnate Word that he is at once fully divine and completely human: that he exists "in two natures," which are permanently distinct but yet inseparable. From one point of view, this statement represents a reiterated denial that there are two substances in Christ. The natures are inseparable because in some sense they *belong to* the divine Word. Both are natures *of* one subject. Neither nature is itself, *qua* nature, a subject or "thing." It is on this distinction that the intelligibility of the *Definition* depends. But at the same time, the natures are abidingly different in the sense that they are recognized in distinguishable sets of properties, each of which is preserved in its logical integrity in the union. Whatever can properly be said of the divine Word can be truly said of the Word incarnate; and whatever sorts of things can properly be said of man can be truly said of the Word incarnate. Thus the governing principle of the *Definition* remains the same as Cyril's. Christ is one in the sense clearly suggested by the language of the Nicene Creed: which is to say, in the sense that the divine Word is the "who," the *substance,* of all that Christ does as well as of all that is said about him; yet at the same time all of Christ's words and actions are human words and actions.

It is important to note here that this "who" is *not* defined psychologically or metaphysically. We have already indicated that the Council does not offer, and its *Definition* does not presuppose, any clear or unambiguous philosophical explanation of the meaning of its nature-substance terminology. One looks in vain to the *Definition* for a declaration in favor of one or more of the theories of the Incarnation which were current in the

fourth and fifth centuries, and which reposed on more or less
philosophical definitions of Christological terminology. Such ra-
tionales of the Person of Christ had been offered, on the Antiochene side, by Theodore of Mopsuestia and by Nestorius; and
Cyril himself, while less consistent and systematic than his opponents, had not failed to suggest a number of quasi-physical
analogies for the Word's becoming flesh. But the Council adopts
none of these proposals. What makes its *Definition* intelligible
is not its advocacy of a particular theory of the Incarnation, but
its tacit insistence on the subject-attribute paradigm as a Christological model. It is true that every individual exposition of its
doctrine (and of course Leo's *Tome* as well) interpreted this
paradigm in a "metaphysical" fashion. But in fact what the
Council offers is not a philosophical explanation of the structure
of the Person of Christ, but a Christological *grammar,* which is
based in the last resort on the logical form of traditional confessional statements about Christ. In order to work with the distinction between "substance" and "nature" in Chalcedonian
terms, what one requires is not a grasp of late Platonist metaphysics, but a commonsense notion of what is involved in distinguishing between the subject of statements about Christ and
the things which such statements say about him.

IV

If this historical account of the character of the Chalcedonian *ekthesis* is acceptable, then it permits us to make some
suggestions about modern interpretation and criticism of the
document. What our historical analysis suggests is that the *Definition*'s terminology can best be treated as *second-order language.*
Functionally considered, the nature-substance terminology reflects
not a metaphysic but something more elementary: a view of the
logical structure of the normal sentence. Hence it becomes intelligible in its Christological use when it is understood not as a
direct account of the constitution of the Person of Christ, but as

a definition of the normative form of any statement about Christ, without consideration of the metaphysical framework which such a direct statement must inevitably presuppose.

This certainly does not mean that it is illegitimate to suggest a first-order philosophical interpretation of the Council's language. It merely means that no such interpretation is *necessitated* by the confession itself, and that in fact, for contemporary purposes, its meaning is better understood when it is taken to be a definition of the proprieties of Christological language.

Interpreted in this sense, the Council's confession can be seen to assert at least four fundamental *dogmata*. First, and most obviously, it insists that all language which refers to Christ (that is, to the incarnate Word) is language about a single, individual subject. Such language does not characterize a class, or a collection, or an organic system of subjects. Sentences which make an assertion about Christ have the same logical character as descriptions or accounts of a particular person.

Second, the *Definition* lays it down that it is both possible and correct to talk about this subject in the same terms one would use to talk about an ordinary human person. Whatever categories of explanation and description are normally used to describe the appearance, the actions, and the words of a man may be used to give an account of the particular actions and words of Christ. Further, such an account of Christ is in principle *complete*. That is to say, all of the phenomena to which we refer when we speak of "Christ" can be described and understood by means of the same sort of language which we use about other men.

But third, the Council's confession demands that this same set of phenomena be described by use of the kind of language which men employ when they talk about God. The words and actions of Christ are to be understood by describing them and explaining them in terms which explicitly refer them to a divine source and characterize them as divine words and actions. Furthermore, this second way of giving an account of Christ must also be taken as in principle complete, in the sense which we have defined above.

Finally, the Council explains that these two ways of giving an account of Christ are not to be confused or equated with each other. They are logically different ways of talking about the same thing; and because both are necessary for an adequate Christian understanding of Christ, neither may be substituted for the other or assimilated to the other.

Obviously there is a sense in which these *dogmata* do not constitute a Christology. They merely specify, by means of a normative description of Christological language, what it is that a Christology sets out to understand and explain. Consequently it is merely wrongheaded to accuse the *Definition* of, for example, losing sight of the figure of the historical Jesus. The *Definition* is not talking about Jesus; it is talking about Christian language about Jesus. An adequate criticism of the Council's confession must address itself, therefore, to this problem, and ask about the clarity and adequacy of the position which the Fathers of Chalcedon took in their description of the logical form of Christological language. Here we can only suggest one or two lines of inquiry which seem to arise naturally out of this understanding of the nature of the Chalcedonian *Definition*.

The first and most obvious problem is that of the logical relation between the two ways of talking about Christ which the Council asserts to be *data* of Christian tradition. There is every reason to suspect that in the era of the Chalcedonian *Definition*, this relation was understood to be one of logical *contrariety*. The two kinds of language used of Christ were not taken to belong to two different orders of discourse, but to be logical opposites within the same order of discourse. It was this fact—and not, I suspect, a "static" conception of the two natures —which gave rise to the absurdities and paradoxes of much later Christology.

For modern theologians, therefore, the Chalcedonian *Defi-*

nition raises in a specific and acute form the question of the logical relation between language about God and "empirical" language. The *Definition* asserts that in the particular case of Christ these two kinds of language are both to be used to give an account of the same *explicandum,* yet that they are logically different and in some way mutually supplementary. Hence the question arises whether—and how—it can make sense to offer two different *kinds* of explanation of the very same event. This is the form which the problem of Christ's "natures" takes for modern theology.

The second difficulty is of a different sort. It arises out of a change in Christological perspective which has come about within the last two hundred years. The Fathers of Chalcedon agreed with Cyril of Alexandria and with a long tradition preceding him that the subject of statements about Christ was simply the divine Word. On the other hand, modern Christology conceives itself to be trying to understand Jesus of Nazareth in his birth, ministry, death, and resurrection. In other words, the Christology of Cyril and the *Definition,* considered from a modern point of view, falsifies the character of the Christological enterprise by in effect distinguishing between the logical subject in statements about Christ and the historical *explicandum* in which the Christological problem has its roots. This procedure may be theologically legitimate, and even necessary, without being methodologically helpful; and the question which it raises is precisely that of the relation between contemporary Christological method and classical Christological confession.

Thus a "linguistic" interpretation of the Cyrillian and Chalcedonian nature-substance terminology does not solve all questions. But it may well assist in their correct definition, and by this means rescue the Council's confession from the contemporary limbo of "metaphysics."

6

Hegel's Logos Christology

BY JAMES E. GRIFFISS

To suggest to theologians that they might once again consider seriously the Christological speculations of German Idealistic philosophy, and especially that of Hegel, would surely strike most people as peculiar. Even though philosophers in recent years have shown renewed interest in Hegel's philosophy,[1] the day has long since passed when Hegel had much influence upon theology. This is all to the good. There can be no serious attempt to revive Hegel among theologians, any more than there can be among philosophers. However, after some years of neglect it is possible once again to see Hegel more clearly and to recognize that there is much in his point of view which we must consider seriously if we are to understand the present state of philosophy, especially that kind called existentialism. It is always necessary for philosophy to reinvestigate its past, to discover its roots once again, in order to understand the questions which are presently being asked. For good or ill Hegel had tremendous influence upon subsequent philosophy, if for no other reason than that he himself set the pattern which the rejection of his philosophy was to take.[2]

In the case of Hegel's theology the matter is more complicated. Although Hegel's influence upon theology had been considerable, the rejection of Hegelianism by theologians was much more thoroughgoing. Part of the reason for this may have been in Hegel's subjugation of theology to philosophy, more evident in his later writings than in his earlier writings; partly also it may have been due to the extraordinary complexity of the Hegelian system, which has tended to obscure whatever contribution Hegel may have made to theology.[3] Unquestionably, however, the main reason for the rejection of the Hegelian synthesis was the attack of Kierkegaard. Kierkegaard's assertion of the radical isolation and alienation of the individual, and consequently his analysis of the paradoxical relation of the individual to God in terms of extreme subjectivity and eternal truth, has been one of the most influential sources of contemporary theology. Against Hegel's abstractness and universal reason Kierkegaard set the necessity of returning always to oneself as existing in the contradiction which existence involves. This is the importance of Kierkegaard's comment in the *Fragment* that we reason from existence, not to it; the self begins with its existential situation.[4] This point of view stands over against the whole point of view of Hegelian philosophy and, fundamentally, alienates Hegelianism and contemporary theology.

However, as Karl Barth has shown in his discussion of Hegel's philosophy of religion, it is not easy to dismiss what Hegel had to say, even though his approach may no longer be possible for us.[5] In virtually all of his philosophical and religious writings, Hegel sought to overcome the radical dualism between the subjective and the objective that had resulted from the critical philosophy of Kant. In Hegel's earliest writings the opposition between God and man expressed itself in terms of an objective religion in which the object of faith stands wholly outside the believer as the believer stands wholly outside the world in which he lives, and a subjective religion in which the objectivity of commands and the natural order is replaced by a religion of spirit. In *The Spirit of Christianity, Love,* and *The Fragment of a System* (this latter name was never used by Hegel and is a misnomer),[6] Hegel is struggling to find some way of saying that God, as the Absolute, is the originative source of himself and of the nature standing in distinction from him without losing the reality of either God or the natural order. In these early writings he did not yet have a method which would enable him to carry out the process of reconciliation[7]; but in his later writings, beginning with *The Phenomenology of Mind,* he attempted to show the dialectical relation between the subjective and the objective in every area of experience and to establish the unity of the two in a third term which would contain them both while allowing for their freedom.

Hegel thus stands between Kant and Kierkegaard in his attempt to find a way to overcome any kind of ultimate separation. For Kant man in his subjectivity is always faced with a radical transcendence of Being which, because he can never determine it in any way, is a transcendent Nothing. Kierkegaard's dialectic involved an acceptance of this transcendent Nothing, and it resulted in the radical isolation of man and the absolute transcendence of God.[8] For Hegel the question always was how to relate to one another both man and God and man and the world in which he lives. In *The Phenomenology of Mind* he arrived at a method by which he thought it would be possible for thought itself to arrive at the mediation of all dualistic forms. It was within this context that Hegel saw the significance of the Christian doctrine of the Incarnation of the Logos in Christ.

The point at which Hegel began *The Phenomenology of Mind* was the reconstruction of Kant's transcendental subject. The knowing subject exercises upon itself a dialectic in which it has for itself an object that it at once distinguishes from itself and relates to itself. The activity of the subject, which Hegel sees as Kant's *Erfahrung,* is a process in which "consciousness is, on the one hand, consciousness of the object, on the other consciousness of itself; consciousness of what to it is true, and consciousness of its knowledge of that truth." [9] What this involves for Hegel is the inclusion of the radically transcendent noumenal object within a process of mediation, in which the subject alienates itself from itself and returns to itself again, knowing itself as its own other.[10] Hegel's development of the Kantian notion of experience is that the meaning or essence of an object (*Wesen*), what it means to be an object, is to be found only within the process of knowing. The essence of the object and the essence which is grasped by the subject in the act of knowledge are not two distinct essences that happen to come into relation with one another: the relationship between an object known and a subject which knows involves some point at which essence itself becomes a mediating term uniting subject and object. Knowing is a process within which a new object and a new subject emerge because both are affected by the dialectic existing between the two.[11] As a new object emerges from the process of experience (the object of experience) so also there emerges a new form of consciousness. In experience both consciousness and its object interact and mutually affect one another; each negates its own untruth but contains the truth of the former state in its new form. This dialectical transformation (*aufheben*) carries forward the succession of the new forms of consciousness with its object. This dialectical process results in *Geist*, which knows itself as itself, absolute knowledge; but the task of *The Phenomenology of Mind* is to show the various forms of *Geist*, and their transformations, until the forms or structures of *Geist* become those of a world.[12] Essential in this whole process, its nerve or life-giving force, is the form of negativity: alienation, otherness, opposition; and it was Hegel's discovery of the meaning of negativity in thought which enabled him to arrive at the dialectical principle. The dialectic sustains itself because the negative never collapses into nothingness; it is always a relation. This is the crucial point for Hegel's philosophical system; the failure to appreciate the force of negativity in Hegel's philosophy resulted in much subsequent misunderstanding of his system.[13]

The idea of the negative power or force is not a new one in Western thought, but Hegel made it a necessary subject of consideration in philosophy by showing the limits within which negativity could be dealt with by rational categories.[14] Hegel states clearly his own conception of the place of the negative principle in thought when he says in the *Phenomenology*:

But the life of the mind is not one that shuns death, and keeps clear of destruction; it endures death and in death maintains its being. It only wins to its truth when it finds itself utterly torn asunder. It is this mighty power, not by being a positive which turns away from the negative, as when we say of anything it is nothing or it is false, and, being then done with it, passes off to something else: on the contrary, mind is this power only by looking the negative in the face, and dwelling with it. This dwelling beside it is the magic power that converts the negative into being.[15]

Originally negativity for Hegel is the bare opposition or dissimilarity which exists between the subject and its object, between ego or consciousness and substance. The process of experience is the course of the development of this opposition on every level where it may manifest itself, until that point is reached where mind has itself for its own object, where thought thinks itself. The Hegelian system thus develops in a circular pattern so that every point within it is not a further linear advance but rather an advance in depth. For this reason the beginning of the dialectic of consciousness, where consciousness is faced simply with the bare opposition of sensory perception, is not intrinsically different from the point when mind meets its own self in absolute knowledge. But at every moment in this development mind meets some form of itself or other as its negative. Indeed the process of experience, which is knowledge, is mind becoming an object for itself, i.e., becoming an other to itself and transcending that otherness.

And experience is called this very process by which the element that is immediate, unexperienced, i.e., abstract—whether it be in the form of sense or of a bare thought—externalizes itself, and then comes back to itself from this state of estrangement, and by so doing is at length set forth in its concrete nature and real truth, and becomes too a possession of consciousness.[16]

Because of Hegel's understanding of the negative moment, which is the self-alienation of mind, that which is other or negative is not lost or abandoned in the process of development. The result of the dialectic is always a new object containing the positive and negative moments, because that is what the object of experience is—the object which is itself *and* its other. (Here is Hegel's development of Kant: the object of experience is that combination of understanding and the given which for Kant is apperception.) Consequently, then, for Hegel "difference itself continues to be an immediate element within truth as such, in the form of the principle of negation, in the form of the activity of Self." [17] The basic principles of Hegel's conception of mediation are here: in the unity of opposites, which is necessary for knowledge itself, there is not a coming together of two strangers, for that would be merely fortuitous, a unity in thought only; rather, because of Hegel's recognition of negativity, the state of contradiction or alienation is seen as *Geist* coming to itself. Mediation is that process in which those opposites standing in a relationship of otherness and alienation to one another discover that the bare opposition of "firstness" must yield to a mutual interrelationship in which unity is pure self-identity in otherness.

At the level of consciousness and reason what Hegel is saying about the dialectic of experience is reasonably clear; it is when he discusses the meaning of *Geist* that one feels he is navigating an uncharted sea. The basic structure of his idea is in his initial statement: "Reason is spirit, when its certainty of being all reality has been raised to the level of truth, and reason is *consciously* aware of itself as its own world, and of the world as itself." [18] Reason is *Geist* in its knowledge of itself, and this means for Hegel that the discussion of *Geist*, although coming at the end of his work, is actually the beginning and the end, because all previous modes of consciousness (in experience itself) are abstractions from it: "they are constituted by the fact

that spirit analyses itself, distinguishes its moments, and halts at
each individual mode in turn." [19] This circular process of the
dialectic is essential to Hegel's analysis of God and the Logos,
because what has been true at every level in the analysis of the
dialectic of experience is an abstraction from what is true about
the nature of God as absolute *Geist*.

The dialectical process through which the reality of God as
Geist is expressed, Hegel states in the following manner: "Essential Being; explicit Self-existence, which is the express otherness of essential Being, and for which that Being is object; and
Self-existence or Self-knowledge *in* that other." [20] The dialectical process of knowledge itself, by means of which the Self comes
to a knowledge of itself, is one in which the consciousness of an
object is seen to be the consciousness of self in its state of alienation from itself. The moment of negativity or alienation is finally
seen as a moment within the reality of God in which what were
before taken as the forms of consciousness are now taken as
forms of a world (*realen Geister*). Self-knowledge requires becoming objective to oneself, alienation or negativity, in order that
one may know oneself.[21] But that process in which we are involved results in what Hegel has called the forms of consciousness. That same process, however, for absolute *Geist* is the process by which the eternal and universal enters into existence and
particularity.

This incarnation of the Divine Being [which Hegel has already
defined as God's immediate and sensuous existence as an individual
human being], its having essentially and directly the shape of self-
consciousness, is the simple content of Absolute Religion. Here the
Divine Being is known as Spirit; this religion is the Divine Being's
consciousness concerning itself that it is Spirit. For spirit is knowledge of self in a state of alienation of self: spirit is the Being which
is the process of retaining identity with itself in its otherness.[22]

In this process of God's knowledge of himself, the second
moment of which Hegel calls the Word, the abstract and uni-

versal becomes concrete and particular; eternal Spirit becomes
an other to itself; it enters existence; it creates a world.[23] From
this point on Hegel develops a speculative interpretation of the
Incarnation and the work of Christ.

Of particular interest and importance in this discussion is
the way in which Hegel tries to understand the significance of
the Logos doctrine. Because his great theological and philosophical interest was to discover the meaning of that kind of unifica-
tion in which difference does not disappear,[24] the notion of the
Logos was especially important, for it is in the structure of language itself, as the Word of God, that mediation is possible.
Hegel's attempt is interesting and important because of the per-
sistent tendency in Christian theology to develop a doctrine of
redemption and reconciliation in which either the reality of God
or the reality of the natural order (i.e., cultural forms) is lost.
Hegel, on the other hand, through his theology of language as
the Word of God attempted to find in cultural forms a mediating
principle.

Cassirer in the course of the development of his own post-
Kantian and post-Hegelian philosophy has seen clearly the significance of language for Hegel. In discussing myth, language,
and art, Cassirer remarks that the essential condition for the
progress of Spirit is that it should place itself in a new relationship to the world of its own creation, i.e., the world of its images
and signs. While still living with them and using them it should
nonetheless know them for what they are. For Cassirer language
expresses this development of Spirit when it leaves behind its
original function of maintaining a simple equivalence between
signifier and signified and becomes, through the emergence of
its own logos, an independent spiritual form. Language and art
are expressions of the progress of Spirit in its self-created world,
and they point to the place where Spirit "not only is and lives
in its own creations, its self-created symbols, but also knows
them for what they are." [25] This, Cassirer says, is precisely the

point of Hegel's attempt in the *Phenomenology*: to show that
cultural reality is to be apprehended and expressed not only as
substance but also as subject.

When Hegel says that in the second part of the *Phenomenology* he is concerned with *realen Geister* as actualities, as forms
of a world, he is attempting to grasp the symbolic forms in and
through which *Geist* comes to know itself. It is for this reason
that language is the medium of the dialectic; it is for thinking
the mediating term between Being and Thought. Because language is finally Logos it makes speculative thought possible. At
the level of consciousness language is the form which *Geist*
takes as the mediating term between Ego and Ego, because it
is both their unity and their alienation from one another; but
at the level of religious consciousness language is crucial because
it points to the symbolic nature of the whole dialectical process,
namely, that language is that in which God reveals himself.

The revelation of God in language occurs for Hegel on two
levels: first, *through* the Word, and second, *as* the Word. The
first form, which includes the cult and the oracle, must be transcended, because in it God is still alien to man and separated
from him. Now God must speak *to* man, and the language in
which God speaks becomes one with its content. This is the
appearance of God as the Logos in revealed religion. Revealed
religion is the immediate setting forth of the life of *Geist* itself
in the three moments which are its wholeness and reality. For
Hegel this means that *Geist* now knows itself as *Geist* (although
immediately, which is the reason for the final section on absolute knowledge), and from this consideration the nature of the
second moment of the process as Logos is developed. Religion
as a whole stands in the dialectical process as self-consciousness,
that is, as consciousness which has made itself object to itself.
It is in this way that consciousness knows itself—that it has
separated itself from itself as its own negative moment. Self-consciousness is the negative moment in the dialectic, consciousness

emptying itself of itself, and in that self-emptying knowing itself is its truth. The same pattern which existed on the level of consciousness now appears again, but here in the twofold relation of God with the world and God with himself.

The dialectic of *Geist* at the level of religion is precisely the eternal dialectic of the divine Being. This is the meaning of religion from the point of view of God's relation to himself. The reality of *Geist* is found in the three moments of its own dialectic with itself. The nature of *Geist* is shown as the process of its own development, the movement within which it returns from its own alienation to itself as the knowledge of itself.[26] The eternal Being separates itself from itself and thereby knows itself as an object in this state of alienation from itself; but the knowledge of itself as an other to itself is at the same moment its unity with itself as *Geist*, for this is what *Geist* is—that which knows itself to be a unity, *an und für sich*. In this process the essential moment is the moment of alienation, for there the absolute Being reveals himself. Essential Being (*Wesen*) sees itself in its otherness to itself as self-existence (*Fürsichsein*), as object for itself which has a reality in itself.[27] Language, then, as the Word, stands as the second moment in an eternal process; it is the negative moment, the moment of otherness, in which *Geist* comes to know itself.

However, the Word is not only the second moment of the divine reality in its relation with itself, but because it is the moment in which God knows himself it is also the eternal revelation of God to men in the form of the Word. This is the revelation to man that the eternal nature of God is *Geist*, that is, self-consciousness. All the names which we apply to God are, Hegel says, predicates based upon this revelation of God's nature. We know God as he is because of his revelation of himself; and his eternal revelation of himself is his reality, self-consciousness which knows itself.[28] At the level of religious consciousness, which is transcended in absolute knowledge, all of this is in the form of images, what Hegel calls *Form des Vorstellens*. The image is the middle term between thought and self-consciousness; it is their synthetic connection; and it is the synthetic connection, the resolution of the other two terms, through being a determinate mode. It is, therefore, in terms of the image that the religious consciousness represents and sees the reality of *Geist*. The image stands to God's revelation of himself for us as the Word: it is the moment of the negative, of otherness, which, as the middle term, mediates the divine nature itself. *Geist* in creating its own spiritual worlds mediates itself through its own symbolic forms. These forms are its own because they are determinate moments in the mediation which is the life of *Geist*; and at the same time they are known by *Geist* because they are *Geist* alienating itself in order to become an object for itself. Language, as the image par excellence, Logos, is the form of otherness, of negativity.

In thus seeing the relationship between language and Logos, Hegel has raised the question of what is implicit in our statement when we speak of things that transcend finite categories. When *Geist* passes beyond reason, as it does when it begins the process of knowing itself, the individual passes explicitly into the universal, and the limitations of finite knowledge are transcended. But the speaking of such things is possible because it is a speaking which is essentially determined by the significance of language itself. *Geist* in its knowing of itself, the eternal life of God in himself and in his revelation, creates its own spiritual forms through which it mediates itself. These spiritual forms, because they are language, Logos, are imaginative representations—symbols—which are in the middle term, the mediating movement, for us who are thinking *Geist*. The language in which we, involved in the process, speak about the process is not a knowledge limited by the limitations of the knowledge of concepts (reason), but one intuitively apprehending the reality which is revealing itself to us. Language, then, is an essential moment in the dialectic of *Geist*, and it is the essential moment for us—the moment which, because it is the middle term, is the synthetic connection of the two extremes.

The meaning of synthetic connection (*synthetische Verbindung*) must consequently be understood in its relation to Kant's synthetic unity of apperception which makes combination possible. Kant extended the synthetic unity of apperception to the transcendental unity of the imagination in the schematism, which is the unity of the concepts of understanding and their objects.[29] The transcendental schema is the *vermittelnde Vorstellung*, which mediates between the two extremes. On this basis then the whole of the second part of the *Phenomenology* is a reworking of the most ancient problem of philosophy and theology—the relation of the universal and the particular, the eternal and the temporal. For Hegel the mediating term is the Logos, for it stands as the negative moment uniting the eternal nature of *Geist* with itself and uniting the universal *Geist* with the individual consciousness.

Consequently, despite the serious limitations of Hegel's view, he does nonetheless stand within the great tradition of Christological thought if for no other reason than that he attempted to take seriously the meaning of Logos. Fundamentally Hegel has tried to establish through his doctrine of the Logos that the structure of the world in which man finds himself is one that is expressive of man's alienation from God and is also one of the bearers of his reconciliation. The ontological structure of reality which Hegel saw as spiritual forms (*Gestalten*) finds its ground in the Logos as the second moment of an eternal process. Certainly in the history of Christian thought the Logos doctrine has meant many things, and it has also raised many problems. But the great strength which it has contributed to the understanding of Jesus Christ is that it has enabled the Church to see the work of Christ in the broadest and most universal possible way. If one takes the Logos of God in terms of the ra-

tional structures of creation, then it is impossible to limit the work
of Christ. The tendency to do this, because of a narrow bibli-
cism, has always been present in Christian history. However, the
broader view which sees the work of Christ in terms of creation
and consummation has always emphasized that God's providence
extends to the whole created order and to everything within it.
The structures of reality, Hegel's spiritual forms, are equally
involved in the process of redemption. Hegel saw this clearly,
and while he did not explicitly develop a doctrine of providence
his whole philosophy of history is based upon the conviction that
the natural order is grounded in the eternal. History, this world
and all that is contained in it, is the working out of God's eternal
purpose. For Hegel it is always a purpose that will be achieved,
not because of a vague optimism, but because the structures of
the natural order are grounded in the being of God. In developing a doctrine of the Logos as the essential moment in the life of
God he has tried to show the meaning of rationality and rational
structures not simply as our thinking about something, what he
called subjective reason, not merely signs of the truth, but as the
forms through which and in which the divine Spirit lives. Thus
for Hegel when we speak of God our language is always Logos:
which is our speaking of God and God's speaking to us.

7

The Conversion of *Diastēma* in the Patristic View of Time

BY L. G. PATTERSON

Recent studies of early Christian views of time differ widely in perspective and approach. Their results—the present state of this subject, so to speak—are correspondingly difficult to summarize. Probably the larger and certainly the better known of two groupings into which such studies fall concerns itself with the conception or conceptions of time in the biblical writings. With regard to the outcome of these studies, it is possible to speak of a growing recognition that no conception of time *as such* is to be found in the writings reflecting the thought world in which Israel lived and in which the main themes of primitive Christian proclamation took shape. Terms which seem to us to suggest at least an implicit conception of time, as we turn back to them over centuries of rational reflection, actually designate configurations of historical events—they employ the notion of "times" in much the same way as we still popularly refer to sets of historical circumstances—rather than any specific understanding of the nature of time itself.[1]

A second grouping of recent studies, probably smaller than the first and certainly the less well known, deals with the subject of time in Patristic literature. Here interest has centered, understandably enough, on the Cappadocian Fathers and Augustine in the fourth century, with whom a serious effort to deal with the subject of time first becomes evident in theological circles, and on the relation of their views to the philosophical notions of time prominent in the age. Since these studies form the background

93

of much that will be said here, it will suffice to note that, in contrast to those just mentioned, the subject under discussion is a
view of time *as such*—as a phenomenon in its own right.[2]

These generalizations, oversimple as they are, must serve
to indicate the scope of the present study. Christian thinking
about the nature of time as a phenomenon in its own right is primarily a product of the confluence of the Gospel and Greek
rationalism in the early Church. With other aspects of Christian
thought as we generally conceive it, it has its origin in the circumstances which obliged early Christians to expound their faith
to themselves and others in the light of the wealth of scientific
knowledge and metaphysical speculation purveyed by the philosophical schools. Its character, contents, and significance are to
be discovered, as in other cases, when it is viewed as part of the
process of the introduction of novel intellectual problems into the
realm of Christian teaching and the interjection of Christianity
as a factor in the history of rational inquiry—a process which
constitutes the history of early Christian thought. In seeking to
deal with such matters in this brief article, it will be possible
for us to do little more than explore the outlines of the Christian
use of the Stoic concept of the time-interval or *diastēma* (var.:
diastasis), which was the principal category of Christian thinking
about time throughout this period. In view of Professor Pittenger's broad interest in matters relating to the origins of Christian
thought, however, it will scarcely be possible to avoid some
reference to the wider ramifications of this study for the understanding of the whole course of theological events of which it
was a part.

I

It must be regarded as a surprising fact that the pioneering
period of Patristic thought—the era bounded by Justin Martyr in
the middle of the second century and Origen in the middle of
the third—was not marked by any significant interest in the nature of time. This does not mean, of course, that Christians of

this period did not have certain assumptions about time. Indeed they shared with their pagan contemporaries the common view of temporality and mutability as unfortunate aspects of the created order which we shall see was at least partly the result of the influence of philosophical ideas. For example, Irenaeus, who was himself no lover of philosophical ideas, argues that God could not have made man perfect from the beginning because created things are necessarily inferior "from the very fact of their later origin" and require long preparation of the sort recorded in the Scriptures before they are ready for the bestowal of "existence without end" by Christ (*Adv. haer.* IV.38.1,3). But while Irenaeus' argument reveals the association of temporality and mutability with the created order deeply lodged in the Greek mind—pagan and Christian—he is fundamentally unconcerned with the nature of time *as such*.

This lack of concern is even more striking where a more accurate knowledge of the philosophical tradition is apparent. Thus Athenagoras, an acute student of the Platonic revival which dominated the philosophical schools of the time, attacks polytheism on grounds occupied jointly with his philosophical colleagues when he argues that idolatry consists in "putting things that are dissoluble and perishable on a level with that which is eternal (*aïdion*)" (*Supp.* 15.5). Subsequently he caustically observes that if the myth of Kronos is defended as a reference to the phenomenon of time, it is still not worthy of worship: "it changes," he says (22.4). Here and elsewhere in Athenagoras' work it is possible to sense the influence of the association of time and cosmic motion characteristic of philosophical discussion. But once again, the nature of time *as such* is not a matter at issue with him.[3]

Most surprising of all is the slight attention paid to time by Origen, unquestionably the most philosophically sophisticated of these writers. Nor is occasion for such attention lacking in his thought. Thus Origen affirms that the divine Word is "always being created (*aei gennētos*)" because it is impossible to attribute

mutability to the relations of spiritual beings (*De princ.* I.2.2)
and also employs the same logic in speculating concerning the
divine creation of the cosmos (I.4.5, cf. I.8.1). Origen's teaching
here is normally described as "eternal creation," but in fact one
reason for later confusion regarding it is precisely that the distinction of the eternal and the temporal plays little part in his considerations. Moreover while Origen elsewhere regards the created
rational natures as subject to mutability in the interests of explaining their defection from God (I.7.1, II.9.1), he again re-
frains from discussing temporality in relation to this problem,
though the attribution of mutability to spiritual beings represents
no less creative a departure from philosophical norms than such
a discussion might have involved. The fact is that where the later
distinction between the eternity of the Godhead and the temporality of even the spiritual elements of the creation might well be
pertinent for Origen, and is often unconsciously supplied by his
interpreters, Origen is himself silent. This does not mean, of
course, that Origen makes no reference to time in his work; but
it does mean that he took no occasion to introduce time as a
decisive element in his thought.[4]

Origen is of particular interest here because it is precisely in
connection with the controversies which arose over various aspects of his revolutionary interpretations of Christian teaching
that the subject of time first assumes importance in the work
of the little-known figure of Methodius, Origen's principal critic
in the latter part of the third century. Moreover Methodius is the
first person in whom we find an adaptation to Christian use of
the Stoic idea of a time-interval or *diastēma* accompanying physical motion.

It is not easy to determine the full extent or character of
Methodius' treatment of time. In his *Symposium* he speaks of
the divine Word as "having been created 'before' (*progen-
nēthenta*)" but nevertheless "timelessly (*achronōs*)" (*Symp.*
VIII.9), and this teaching corresponds to the formula in which
he frequently refers to "the Word (existing) before the ages (*pro*

aiōnōn)" (e.g., *Symp.* VII.1, *De cibis* XII.4, *De res.* II.10.2). In
the light of the later exposition of such language by the early
Arians, on whom Methodius exercised an influence, it is almost
certain that he means here to assign the Word to an undifferentiated period of time prior to the time intervals accompanying
the movements of the present cosmos. Though important features
of the early Arian treatment of creation are anticipated in Methodius' attack on Origen's speculations regarding the creation
of the cosmos (*De creatis* XI), it does not seem that Methodius'
own view of the creation of the Word is anti-Origenist in inspiration. Indeed it seems more likely that it is actually an attempt to
restate the teaching of Origen in somewhat different form which
leads Methodius to introduce the notion of the time interval in
this area of his thought. Even so Methodius bears witness to the
origin of Christian interest in time in the aftermath of Origen's
work, as well as providing a clue to the mysterious relation between early Arian ideas and revisions of Origenist teaching.[5]

It is in his work on the resurrection (*De resurrectione*)
that Methodius develops his view of time most fully in his criticism of Origen's argument that the physical bodies of men are
essentially transitory and consequently unable to participate in a
resurrection at the last day. No one in touch with the medical
science of the day could avoid the force of Origen's argument,
and Methodius was compelled to seek rational grounds for Christian belief in the resurrection which would take account of the
evidence of physical change to which Origen points. He finds
these grounds in the destructive character of time, "which never
stands still but always moves and tears down created things
with its longer and shorter intervals" (*De res.* II.25.2).

Nevertheless, Methodius argues, the cessation of the movement of these time-intervals will bring with it the transformation
of the transitory body into a permanent body existing in an
undifferentiated present time:

There are altogether three intervals of time, past, present, and
future. And for this reason the Lord spent that many days in the

earth as a symbol, teaching that when these intervals of time shall be fulfilled, then shall come our resurrection, which is the beginning of the future age and the end of this. For in the age to come (*en aiōni*) there is neither past nor future, but only the present (II.25.8).

Behind this argument is Methodius' view that God's design for the perfection of the creation necessitates the completion of the human plenitude by procreation and the fluctuations of the physical order which it entails (*De res.* II.20-23, cf. *Symp.* II.1-2, 5-6; IX.1-4). Thus his full answer to Origen is that the correlative phenomena of time and physical motion, which render the body transitory, are temporary conditions necessitated by God's design: the resurrection of the body is not only possible, it will be the natural result of the fulfillment of this design.

Methodius' argument must strike us as weak and speculative. But it should not be overlooked that it is a serious attempt to explain time and change as positive rather than purely negative phenomena. In any case, the character of the notion of time which he employs here, as well as the difficulties which attend its use, can best be judged in the light of the discussion of time in the contemporary philosophical scene.

II

The best-known contribution to the discussion of time in later Greek philosophy is the revolutionary effort of Plotinus to explain time as an internal condition of the soul—"the life of the soul as it passes from one experience to another" (*Enn.* III.7.11, 41). For the most part, however, the focus of contemporary discussion, as Plotinus' own strictures against it show, was the traditional association of time and cosmic motion. For Plato the phenomenon of time had appeared simply as the movement of the heavenly bodies itself (*Tim.* 38B, cf. 41E, 42D). His famous figure of time as a "moving image of eternity" (37D) is simply an effort to relate time so conceived to his mythological picture of the purposeful ordering of the cosmos. To a large extent, contemporary discussion was naturally confined to the exposition of this view (cf. Plutarch, *Plat. quaest.* 1007A-D). But later views of the association of time and cosmic motion were also remembered in the period. For Aristotle time had appeared as the "number" or "measure of motion" (*Phys.* IV.11, cf. VIII.1, *De caelo* I.9)—the numerical aspect of that motion. Moreover for the Stoic teachers Zeno and Chrysippus, redefining Aristotle's formula along lines determined by the materialism of the Stoa, time had become an incorporeal but substantial reality which was not merely a product of motion but something measured by it. Thus there is a single "interval of the motion of the cosmos" which accompanies the whole of cosmic motion, though this interval is divided into past, present, and future segments as it accompanies the motion of the articulated cosmos.[6] The scattered remains of the contemporary philosophical scene show various instances of the adaptation of Aristotelian and even Stoic themes. The Platonist Albinus, for example, interprets the figure of the "moving image of eternity" as meaning that time is a "measure of the permanence of the eternal cosmos" produced by an "interval of its motion" (*Did.* XIV). The Jewish Platonist Philo sees time as an "interval of the motion of the cosmos" (*De opif. mundi* VII.26), of which God is creator insofar as he is also the creator of the cosmos which produces it (*Quod deus immut.* 6). In each case a radical Platonization of Aristotelian and Stoic ideas has occurred simply because time is a feature of the physical side of the Platonic dualism. Moreover in both cases the substantial reality with which Zeno and Chrysippus invested time is either underplayed or abandoned since the materialism to which they were committed is no longer an issue.

Even this brief review of what is an exceedingly complicated phase of later Greek philosophical discussion should shed some light on the views of Methodius and the beginnings of Christian interest in time to which he bears witness. We see here the almost universal association of time with cosmic motion which is reflected in the oblique references to time in second-century and early-third-century Christian literature. But the reverse of this situation, so to speak—the lack of association of time with history—helps to explain why these Christians, in the course of explaining the Gospel to their philosophical contemporaries, were not confronted with the issue of time as a problem. Indeed, time and cosmic motion could not become important and serious theological issues until Origen seriously questioned the relation of the Christian teaching on creation and resurrection to the accepted philosophical assumptions about the cosmos. It was in the scramble to deal with these issues in the later third century that serious thinking about time originated.

So far as Methodius is concerned, this review should help to render his eclectic use of philosophical ideas intelligible. Despite his obvious use of the Stoic notion of time, he remains a Platonist. Though his particular views are not always clear, God and his creation are identified with the Platonic spiritual and physical realms.[7] Moreover, for him as for Albinus and Philo, time and motion are characteristics of the physical cosmos. At one crucial point, however, Methodius differs from both his Stoic sources and his Platonic contemporaries. He adapts the notion of the independent existence of time to a special purpose which can only be explained by the circumstances in which he finds himself as a Christian. He seeks to understand it as an instrument of divine providence as he wrestles with Origen's argument concerning the essentially transitory nature of the body. For this there is no philosophical precedent.[8]

At the same time that this special use of the time interval is revealed, however, the problem which it encounters becomes clear. The adverse judgment against time and change which are everywhere apparent in the philosophical world cannot easily be overcome. It remains in the argument that these aspects of the present situation of man are indeed destructive but are merely temporary expedients employed in view of the ultimate fulfillment of the divine purpose which necessitates them. This problem was to become far more acute when aspects of Methodius' argument were employed later by a mind far more conversant with the contemporary philosophical scene than his.

III

Methodius does no more than mark the beginning of early Christian thinking about time. It is with the Cappadocian Fathers and Augustine that we first encounter time as a major theological issue. That Methodius exercised a surprising influence on the work of his illustrious successors is owing not so much to his own profundity as to the fact that he anticipated some of the ways in which the vital interests of Christianity were bound to reveal themselves in this area.

The Cappadocian treatment of time constitutes a nice example of the independent but interrelated development of common themes which characterizes the thought of this surprising triad of great theologians. Here we must limit our consideration to the views of Basil and his brother Gregory of Nyssa, merely remarking that Gregory of Nazianzus adds little to the work of his *confrères* in this area.[9]

It is with Basil that we first encounter the two quite particular connections in which the issue of time arose for the Cappadocians: (1) their insistence on the eternity of the divine Word as one of the members of the Godhead against the resurgent Arianism of their day, and (2) their discussion of the relation of time to the progress of the soul toward perfection. In the first connection, Basil asserts the true eternity (*to aïdion*) of the Godhead in uncompromising fashion in his attack on the Arian theologian Eunomius (*PG* XXIX.608C). However, his only other sortie in this area is his rather specialized attack on remarks of Eunomius which seem to equate time simply with the movements of the heavenly bodies. Time, Basil insists, is not physical motion itself but "the interval . . . by which all motion is measured" (560B). The argument is interesting as showing the continued use of the Stoic formula by the Cappadocian group, though in fact it neither gets at the heart of the matters at issue with the Arians nor fully reveals Basil's own position regarding time.

Basil has more to say about time in the second connection mentioned above. In the first of his unfinished series of *Hexaëmeral Orations,* he speaks of a first creation of spiritual nature— the ranks of angels—whose life is "beyond time, 'aeonic,' and eternal" (*PG* XXIX.13A). With this is contrasted a subsequent physical creation, which was necessary as a "school and training ground where the souls of men could be taught and a home for beings destined to be born and die," and with which the "succession (*diexodos*) of time" is associated (13B). This treacherous passage was more than sufficient to raise the specter of Origen's controversial teaching concerning the original equality of rational natures and the subsequent embodiment of those which had turned from God, but it is truly difficult to say how Basil himself meant it to be understood. This is not the only place where Basil speaks of the angelic life as lived in an *aiōn* which is different from both the true eternity of God and the time interval that accompanies physical existence (cf. *Hom. in Ps.,* PG XXIX.388C), and we have already encountered the notion of the time interval itself in his attack on Eunomius. But Basil is quite silent, perhaps from both prudence and honest bemusement, as to the origin of the souls now existing in time and the state for which they are destined.

The question of Basil's Origenism is by no means the only issue here. As Professor Otis has shown in recent articles, the Cappadocian insistence on the infinity and inaccessibility of the members of the Godhead paved the way for a novel view of the spiritual life as an endless progress toward God which leads neither to simple merger with the divine nor to the satiety which Origen had supposed to be involved in the soul's defection from God—but which Origen also found to be the chief stumbling block to an intelligible explanation of its finally attaining stability in a "restoration of all things." [10] But this notion is an underlying

issue here, since the precondition of the progress of the soul is a
life free from the disruptions of ordinary time—like that of the
angelic *aiōn*. For one reason or another, among them doubtless his
failure to complete this work, it is hard to comprehend what
Basil's resolution of this problem was. However, he does reveal the
difficulties which stood in the way of finding a resolution of it.
For him the time interval is a purely negative phenomenon; but
at the same time, the possibility of regarding man as destined for
an angelic life had been foreclosed, so to speak, by reaction to
Origen's views. We may speculate that it was not only Basil's
death but also the fact that he had no more to say on this matter
which explains his failure to complete this work with the crucial
treatment of the creation of man on the sixth day.[11]

Gregory of Nyssa pressed the attack against resurgent Arianism in his reply to Eunomius' answer to his recently deceased
brother. In his own polemic, he reasserts the true eternity of the
Word or Son and offers a far more comprehensive treatment of
the issue of time. It is blasphemous and unintelligible to introduce
ideas of "before" and "after" into the divine life, he insists, since
time comes into being with the creation and "the whole temporal
interval" is the work of the Son (*PG* XLV.357B). Nor is it possible to speak of an infinite time interval in connection with the
Son, since the creation alone exists as an ordered sequence measured "by the interval of the aeons" (364D). Thus the divine nature "is not in time, but time flows from it; whereas the creation,
starting from a manifest beginning, journeys onward to its proper
end through the time-intervals (*dia tōn chronikōn diastēmatōn*)"
(365B). It is the most obvious of truths that "the creator established the aeons and the space which occurs within them as a
container for all that was to be brought into existence" (367D).

There are notable differences within the general similarities
linking Gregory's attack on the Arian problem with Basil's. As
Balthasar noted,[12] Gregory's inclusion of the entire creation
within the time intervals allows no clear distinction between the
time of spiritual and physical beings, and the terminology just

used certainly suggests an equation between the "aeons" and the
time intervals which accompany physical motion. Moreover, in
a part of the work written several years later, Gregory says that
all created things whatsoever are defined by their temporal intervals (795C) and adds that this in no way hinders the angels or
souls of men in their progress toward eternity (*aïdion*) (796D).
The clue to Gregory's modifications of Basil's views is unquestionably to be sought in the fact that this work was written in
close conjunction with the two treatises—*On the Making of
Man* (*De hominis opificio*) and *On the Soul and the Resurrection* (*De anima et resurrectione*)—in which he sought to resolve
the problems raised by Basil's unfinished *Hexaëmeral Orations*.
The contents and relations of these two works, which are certainly among Gregory's most remarkable contributions to Patristic
thought, are studies in themselves, and we must drastically limit
our consideration to the matters at issue here.

    Gregory's immediate problem in his *On the Making of Man*
is that of completing Basil's unfinished work in such a way as to
remove the stigma of Origenism from his views. The underlying
problem, however, is that of explaining embodied life as a stage
on the way to the perfection of the soul. The heart of the work
(chaps. 16 ff.) is the argument that man was embodied from
the beginning because God foresaw that his fall would necessitate
the completion of the human plenitude by a process of procreation slower than that employed by the angels. This present life
(chaps. 22 ff.) involves the temporality and mutability required
by the slow completion of this plenitude. But both time and
change will end with its completion, and the stable bodies of the
resurrection will appear:

    God also foreknew the time coextensive with the creation of
men, so that the ordering of time should be adapted for the appearance of the predetermined number of souls, and that the surging
motion of time should cease when the human plenitude is no
longer produced by it, and that when the formation of men should

cease, time itself should be brought to an end with it, and then should take place the "restoration of all things" and . . . humanity should be changed from the corruptible and earthly to the impassible and eternal (*aidion*) (*PG* XLIV.205C).

Gregory's second work, *On the Soul and the Resurrection*, has all the earmarks of a revision of the argument of the first. The curious notion of the relation of embodiment and divine fore-knowledge of sin is omitted, and a variety of arguments concerning the certainty of the resurrection and its physical character are revised in a more spiritual direction. However, the main point of the earlier work is repeated. Corporeal existence presently undergoes changes required by the production of the human plenitude, but an undisturbed life awaits both soul and body at its completion (*PG* XLV.125-129). This life will appear when the resurrection occurs simultaneously with the cessation of the whole time interval (*PG* XLVI.236A).

Gregory's argument in both these works involves the adaptation of the argument of Methodius along lines indicated by Gregory's own theological commitments and a far greater philosophical knowledge.[13] Thus Gregory elaborates the basic Methodian notion of successive time and physical motion as essential to the formation of the human plenitude by including the whole of the created order, spiritual and physical, within its scope— all waits on the fulfillment of this phase of the divine plan.[14] On the other hand, Gregory sees the end of this process not as a final eschatological "aeon" or stable time interval but as emergence into an eternal existence beyond time itself. What Gregory has thus done is to use the Methodian view as a means of counter-acting the negative view of time found in Basil's work and of associating time with the progress of the soul toward perfection.

The Cappadocian treatment of time reflects the breadth of philosophical knowledge possessed by all the Cappadocians and informing all features of their thought. Fundamentally, however, it is determined by the classic association of time and physical

motion, by the earlier Christian use of the concept of the time
interval conveyed to them with the other issues of the Arian
controversy, and—in the case of Gregory of Nyssa in particular—
by the earlier adaptation of this concept by Methodius. Their
thought constitutes a further exploration of the significance of
the concept of the time interval at the hands of people who
possessed among themselves a knowledge of contemporary ideas
equal to that of Origen.[15] It is just because of this latter fact that
the Cappadocians reveal even more clearly than Methodius the
difficulty which Christians faced in this area of their thought.
Despite the efforts of both Basil and Gregory in their several ways
to constitute from time and change vehicles for the fulfillment
of God's plans, neither is able to escape the negative judgment
which had been passed on these phenomena by philosophical
writers. In both cases, but notably in Gregory's because of his
attempt to give positive significance to time and change, it is
clear that the only basis for the progress of the soul is an eternal
state that is difficult to distinguish from that of the divine nature
itself. A further step in the direction in which they sought to
move became possible only with the emergence of this problem
beyond the confines of the philosophical world in which they
lived.

IV

It is even more dangerous to attempt to deal briefly with
Augustine than to pass such swift judgment on the Cappadocian
Fathers. Not only does the question of the extent of Augustine's
familiarity with Greek philosophical and theological writings—
and hence his relation to these developments—remain an open
one, but a whole new series of considerations introduces itself
with his appearance as a representative of the Latin thought
world which had already left its imprint in adaptations of pagan
and Christian Greek thought forms over centuries before his time.
But recent work on Augustine's view of time, and especially
Professor Callahan's study of his use of Basil's concept of the time

interval, makes it possible to relate his view of time with the issues of early Christian thinking on this subject without extensive preliminaries.[16]

It has commonly been held that Augustine's definition of time, in his *Confessions,* as a certain "distention of the soul" is fundamentally derived from Plotinus' view of time as the successive dimension of the life of the soul. The definition is a familiar one: "inde mihi visum est nihil esse aliud tempus quam *distentionem*: sed cuius rei, nescio, et mirum, si non ipsius *animi*" (*Conf.* XI.26). What is now clear from Callahan's work is that this definition is in important respects developed in the light of Basil's assertion that time is an interval measured by cosmic motion. Thus the turning point of the lengthy dialectical treatment of time (*Conf.* XI.11-30), at which Augustine passes from his reflections on the subjective apprehension of the phenomenon to a positive definition of its nature, consists of a discussion of time as a means of the measurement of cosmic motion which is actually an independent presentation of the Basilian argument against Eunomius mentioned earlier (*Conf.* XI.23; cf. Basil, *Contra Eunomium* I.22, PG XXIX.557C-560C). The conclusion reached by this argument—that time is a *distentio* separate from but related to motion—contributes an important element to the definition of time that Augustine finally reaches. His definition of time as *distentio* has two aspects: the independence of time from motion is asserted in a new way by reference to its relation to the soul, and time itself is assured an objective frame of reference by the fact of its function as a measurement of motion.[17]

Another aspect of Augustine's treatment of time in *Confessions* is its suffusion with his interest in historical events and the clash of wills which constitute them, rather than in cosmic motion and the physical change which underlies it. The immediate occasion for Augustine's interest in time is his meditation on the relation between the eternity of God and the temporal successiveness of human life (XI.11). But this meditation ultimately arises from his discussion of memory, from which it is

determined that God is not encountered through the memory in
which the events of the past are stored but in the living present
that is a segment of the total course of time through which God
is always related to human existence (X.14-16). In its turn this
discussion springs from Augustine's rehearsal of the events of his
own life, through which God had acted to convert his will—the
real substance of his *Confessions*.

It is doubtless a long way from the theme of the early books
of *Confessions* to the discussion of time near its end, but the two
are intimately related. Not only does Augustine arrive at the
question of the nature of time as a consequence of his concern
with the course of events of his own life, but he reveals this
primary concern by the context in which he finally places the
definition of time as *distentio*. It is at this point that Augustine
institutes his comparison between the succession of happenings
which form a human life and the singing of a psalm. The analogy
between the passage of each syllable of the psalm from expectation to memory, he says, holds good for the activities which constitute each single life and the life of the whole race: "in tota
vita hominis, cuius partes sunt omnes actiones hominis . . . in
toto saeculo filiorum hominis, cuius partes sunt omnes vitae
hominum" (XI. 28).

Augustine concludes with the remarkable image of Christ
taking hold of his hand in the midst of the passing events of his
life; and he prays that he may go on to set himself free from the
distraction of successiveness and live the rest of his life concentrated on his heavenly calling and on the unchanging divine
delight which awaits him there: "non distentus sed extentus,
non secundum distentionem sed secundum intentionem . . .
ad palmam supernae vocationis, ubi audiam vocem laudis et con-
templer delectationem tuam nec venientem nec praetereuntem"
(XI.29). The significance of the play on words (*distentio, distentus, distentionem*) cannot be overlooked. It does not mean, of
course, that Augustine identifies time itself with the events of life.

But it does show that he remains concerned with time as perceived in connection with the successive character of the events of life.

Thus Augustine brings a new association of ideas to the discussion of time, which is nothing less than the association of time with historical event rather than cosmic motion. As in other cases in which the Latin mind is satisfied to operate through the rational formulations inherited from the Greeks, Augustine is content to pursue his reflections on the inner apprehension of time and its external frame of reference in the manner of his Greek models. But in the end he gives a different meaning to them, since the real phenomena with which time is associated in his mind are the events of his life and the clash of wills—the struggle between himself and his own better self, and between himself and God—which he has witnessed there. For Methodius and the Cappadocians time and motion remain fundamentally unfortunate characteristics of cosmic existence, but for Augustine it is the sinful distraction of the soul by the successiveness of life which is the real misfortune; and for him redemption lies not in the eventual emergence of the soul beyond time and change as such but in the redirection of the will away from this life toward that offered by God.

It is impossible to proceed here with a consideration of ways in which the transformation of ideas of time seen in *Confessions* is continued in Augustine's later writings—especially in his study of the course of human history in the second part of the treatise *On the City of God*. It must suffice to suggest that important features of his treatment of time in the latter connection bear a suspicious resemblance to the views of Gregory of Nyssa rather than Basil. This is especially true of the discussion of the succession of time intervals and accompanying cosmic motions which attend the progress of the creation (*De civ. dei* XI.6) and of the explanation of time and motion as related to the fulfillment of the human plenitude (XII.12-16, 19-20). However, the theme

of the work did not require extensive consideration of the subject of time as such. Augustine is here absorbed in a description
of the sinful formation of the earthly city in the lower reaches of
the creation (XI-XIV), the subsequent establishment of Israel as
a continuing witness to the existence of the heavenly city in its
midst (XV-XIX), and the final appearance of the Church as an
eschatological anticipation of the heavenly city as it will be per-
fected at the end of history (XX-XXII). The important point to
note is simply that the whole cosmological discussion in which
Augustine's principal references to time occur in this work is
designed as an exposition of the plans of God for his creation,
into which the fall of angels and men and the events flowing
from them have intruded themselves. It is in this way primarily
that the work constitutes another illustration of the association of
inherited notions of the relation of time and cosmic motion with
the course of historical events.[18]

But these later developments add little to the main purposes
of this study. Augustine stands at a point of transition in Christian thinking about time, and his work provides us with the perspective which such a point of transition always affords. In
contrast to older interpretations of his views, recent studies have
served to point up the continuity rather than the discontinuity
between his understanding of time and earlier Christian treat-
ments of the subject. His work continues and concludes the use
of the concept of the time interval as a vehicle of Christian
thinking about time in this period. Also, it involves a further
transformation of this concept beyond that which had occurred
in Greek Christian circles. The Greek attempt to make time an
instrument of the divine purpose faced insoluble difficulties
because of the negative connotations possessed by the ideas of
time and change in the philosophical tradition of which they were
heirs. But these difficulties were absorbed, so to speak, in the
course of Augustine's attempt to discuss time as a dimension of
the world of person, will, and event which his Latin cultural
heritage required him to explore.

With Augustine's work we have arrived at a point from which we can survey the implications of early Christian thinking about time more generally. An interest in "times" as concatenations of events is a different thing from an explicit definition of "time" in terms of event. The latter began to emerge only as the result of an epoch of rational reflection in which the eschatological proclamation of the Gospel, the vital problems of Greek scientific investigation and metaphysical speculation, and the historical orientation of Latin thinking—a unique cultural phenomenon possessing affinities with both—all played decisive parts. Our own theological reflection on the relation of time to history is, indeed, in large part the result of the impact of modern secular historical and philosophical considerations which are profoundly but indirectly related through the continued involvement of Christianity in intellectual affairs over a much longer period than we have considered here. It should be added that our current notions of historical event have an analogous origin, though the limitations of space have made it impossible to consider this matter here. But if it is true that the association of time with historical event is the product of a course of ideas only the beginnings of which are to be found in the period here concerning us, it is also true that those beginnings are to be found there— in the confluence of the great constitutive forces, Hebraic, Greek, and Latin, which lie at the beginning of the vast intellectual history from which we cannot detach ourselves today.

8

The Jungle of Jordan

BY KENNETH J. WOOLLCOMBE

In the spring of 1948, Dr. Austin Farrer devoted the seventh of his Bampton Lectures to a study of poetry and its resemblance to prophecy; the *leit-motiv* of the lecture was a striking and memorable sentence: "The Muse is in the melting-pot, and I cannot see what is happening to her." [1] In the spring of 1965, however, it is theology rather than poetry which appears to be in the melting-pot, and none of us can see very clearly what is happening to *her*. During the early 1960's two notable books demonstrated that we are witnessing a sort of theological revolution. On the one hand, John A. T. Robinson's *Honest to God* represents a swing of the pendulum back and away from the transcendentalism of Karl Barth to something very like the immanentism of the Idealists fifty years ago. On the other hand, Paul Van Buren's *The Secular Meaning of the Gospel*—in spite of the author's claim that he agrees with much of what the Bishop of Woolwich has to say[2]—represents a swing of the pendulum in the opposite direction beyond and forward from the transcendentalism of Barth. Van Buren has deliberately pushed God off the map entirely and devised a theology which excludes him.

Consequently students of theology find themselves in a bewildering quandary: should they side with Robinson or with Van Buren, or should they try to hold their ground, in the hope that the incoming tide will not entirely surround it or wash it away? It is the purpose of the present essay to show that there is something to be said for Anglican theologians holding their ground, not out of conservatism or sheer fright but because there are, within the traditional framework of Anglican theology, certain basic assumptions which need to be reaffirmed.

Van Buren observes[3] that the chief difference between his work and that of Robinson lies in their choice of theological method: Van Buren takes Christology as a starting point, and then proceeds to theology; Robinson moves in the opposite direction. In this respect the former is characteristically Barthian, the latter Anglican. But if Anglican theology begins with God, it begins with God transcendent and immanent, whose immanence requires him to be transcendent and vice versa—a contention that will be familiar to those who are familiar with the books of Archbishop William Temple. And there's the rub: the transcendence of Van Buren's God, if he exists, does not require him to be immanent, nor does the immanence of Robinson's God require him to be transcendent. For example, Van Buren defines prayer as "speaking to God," [4] as might any transcendentalist. But the secular meanings which Van Buren proceeds to give to prayer are *concern for others* or *reflection upon oneself,* and these secular meanings not only preclude the principal purpose of prayer, which is to give God an opportunity of speaking to *us,*[5] but also more specifically exclude his immanence. Similarly Robinson's stress upon the immanence of God leads him into the characteristic problem of the immanentist—that of distinguishing, in prayer, between what God says to him, and what he says to himself. That the Bishop of Woolwich has had to wrestle with this difficulty is obvious from the fifth chapter of *Honest to God;* whether he has surmounted it successfully is less obvious. For it is not clear that he has grasped the fact that the transcendence of God "is compatible with the deepest immanence; the two are in fact different ways of looking at the same thing. Just because God is other than all things he is free from the sundering limitations of every definite thing and can be immediately present to all things everywhere." [6]

If Anglican students of theology are to find an answer to

their present quandary and, in doing so, to make a balanced critical assessment of Van Buren and Robinson, it behooves them to take the doctrines of divine transcendence and immanence off the shelf where J. R. Illingworth left them in 1912; it is also necessary that they should see their current problems in some sort of historical perspective. To do this the English have to cast their minds back to 1935, because it was about thirty years ago that English theological studies, so to say, "froze"; and although the thaw has begun to set in, it is by no means complete. Shortly after the death of Charles Gore in 1932,[7] English theology came to a standstill, whereas Continental theology kept up its momentum until the outbreak of World War II. Since the end of the war theological studies have made much slower progress in Britain than in the United States or Europe, with the result that much of what Robinson and others are saying is fresh to us, but stale to our transatlantic colleagues. It is also significant that although the philosophy of process was a valuable tool in the hands of the theologians of the 1930's, there have been few able or bold enough to use it in the debate with the linguistic analysts since 1945. Reluctant to import foreign ideas, equally reluctant to develop ideas which originated in its own territory, English theology has become steadily less adventurous and more historical.

It was difficult for an Englishman to know what to make of the world in 1935. The worst years of the depression were over; the Cunarder *Queen Mary* had been launched; production had begun to increase, unemployment to decrease. It was the year of the Silver Jubilee of King George V; on Monday, May 6, 1935, the London *Daily Mail* was printed on silver paper, and showed the British empire at its most spectacular: bonfires and fireworks, processions, pageants, and tattoos, a service in St. Paul's with all the glitter of ceremony in a glorious English spring. Who could be blamed for mistaking the sunset of an old world for the dawn of a new?

And yet there were signs which forbade optimism: 1935

was the year of Mussolini's invasion of Abyssinia and the year of Martin Niemöller's first imprisonment. The first flood of Jewish refugees had arrived in London to seek new homes and opportunities for work. Karl Barth was obliged to leave Germany for refusing to take the oath of allegiance to Hitler. Nevertheless these premonitions of the gathering storm were discerned by only a few, like the distinguished preacher who was moved to preach on the text: "If thou hast run with the footmen, and they have wearied thee, then how canst thou contend with horses? And if in the land of peace, wherein thou trustedst, they wearied thee, then how wilt thou do in the swelling of Jordan?" (Jer. 12:5, AV). Evidently he had not mistaken the signs of the times, but he was of the minority. The majority enjoyed myopic isolation from the rest of the world.

The Church of England has been described as "rather like an old lady who gets flustered in the middle of a crowded street. She hears a confusion of voices; she sees a number of different ways; she begins to doubt why she has come, and still more where she is meant to go. In the end, to the great danger of herself and others, she is tempted to stay where she is." [8] It is a highly unflattering description, to be sure, but it could hardly be bettered as an allegory of the English Church in the '30's. The high churchmen were getting higher, the low churchmen were getting lower, and the broad churchmen were getting broader. By which I mean to say that after the death of Charles Gore those who advocated the Liberal Catholicism for which he stood tended to lose ground to those who advocated a greater degree of accommodation to Roman theology and practice. Liberal Evangelicalism was beginning to give way to Conservative Evangelicalism (or Fundamentalism). The broad churchmen, or modern churchmen as they preferred to be called, were beginning to lose their bearings and their sense of direction altogether. Dean Inge may have put his finger on the reason for this when he said on resigning from the Deanery of St. Paul's in 1934: "A devout Christian may be a Liberal Protestant or a Liberal Catholic; he can hardly be a Liberal without any qualification." [9] At all events, what had begun in the modernist movement as a fine and necessary protest against the formalism and fixity of both Anglo-Catholic and Evangelical theology was degenerating into "Each man for himself and God for us all."

But in spite of increasing division within the Church of England there was one *theologoumenon* common to all the parties, though it is possible that they were unaware of it, and certain that the chroniclers of recent developments in Anglicanism have paid insufficient attention to it. Their religion was based upon devotion to the humanity of Christ: they could all say with complete sincerity the prayer of St. Richard of Chichester: "O holy Jesus, most merciful redeemer, friend and brother, may I know thee more clearly, love thee more dearly, and follow thee more nearly." The high churchman could say it, as he said the *Anima Christi*, because the pattern of his prayer life was based upon a Jesus-centered spirituality of medieval origin (excellently described by Dr. G. L. Prestige in the last of his Bampton Lectures, *Eros: or Devotion to the Sacred Humanity*[10]). The low churchman could say it, because it expressed in the form of a prayer what he meant when he said that he had accepted Christ as his personal Saviour. The modern churchman could say it, because, in the words of Dr. Bethune-Baker, "In getting to know Jesus we get to know God. . . . but only by knowing him always as man. . . . My concept of God is formed by my conception of Jesus." [11]

Devotion to the humanity of Christ was the highest common *religious* factor in the Anglicanism of the '30's; furthermore, as Bethune-Baker testified, it had a pervasive and radical influence upon English theology. Only by understanding and appreciating the strength and depth of this religious factor shall we understand and appreciate the sense of shock which Anglicans experienced when they began to realise some of the new directions which theology appeared to be taking in 1935—in particular, Neo-orthodoxy and Form Criticism.

Continental transcendentalism held no immediate attractions for Anglicans, whose tradition gave them a nicer perception of the balance between transcendence and immanence in the doctrine of God than Neo-orthodox theologians had in the early days of the movement. Nevertheless the works of Barth and Brunner were being translated into English in the '30's. Sir Edwyn Hoskyns published a translation of Barth's commentary on Romans in 1933; the English translation of the first volume of the *Kirchliche Dogmatik* appeared in 1936, that of Brunner's *Der Mittler* in 1934. Furthermore they were being read by a few of the more discerning theologians and graduate students, though not, as in Scotland, by undergraduates. The Archbishop of Canterbury has admirably described the shock that they administered to theologians:

> It was the "shock" of facing, with a starkness we had not seen before, the contrasts: God-Man, Creator-Creature, God-the World. It was the "shock" of realizing that our knowledge and grasp of divine truth can be totally perverted through becoming a thing of "ours," a possession to enjoy and defend, so that ultimately it witnesses to ourselves and not to God. The difference came home between faith on the one hand, and piety and religion on the other.[12]

The crux of the Archbishop's assessment of the situation is in the last sentence—the difference between faith on the one hand, and piety on the other. Anglican piety was based upon devotion to the humanity of Christ, and this purely *religious* factor had become lynch-pin of *theology*, taking precedence over the basic doctrines of God, Faith, and Revelation. For example, Professor N. P. Williams, a high churchman, could make the astonishing statement that if the Virgin Birth were to be disproved, he "would at once abandon not merely the belief in the Virgin Birth, but all the rest of Catholic Christianity as well." [13]

In a way that was quite uncharacteristic of classical Anglicanism theology had become devotional and Christocentric; its traditional theocentric bastions were neglected or deserted. Anglicans, therefore, could only descry blasphemy in Barth's notorious dictum, "Jesus Christ in fact is also the Rabbi of Nazareth, historically so difficult to get information about, and when it is got, one whose activity is so easily a little commonplace alongside more than one other founder of a religion, and even alongside many later representatives of his own 'religion.' " [14] It seemed to them to put a charge of dynamite under the foundations of the Church.

If the form-critical movement had impinged upon Anglican scholarship at an earlier date, no doubt it would have been better prepared to assimilate what Barth had to say. But English universities were slow to adopt the new technique for the analysis of the Gospels; for example, Martin Dibelius' *Die Formgeschichte des Evangeliums,* written in 1919, was not translated into English until 1933, and Rudolf Bultmann's *Die Geschichte der Synoptischen Tradition,* written in 1921, did not appear in English until 1963. Admittedly Sir Edwyn Hoskyns and Noel Davey had published *The Riddle of the New Testament* in 1931, but as Vincent Taylor rightly observed in the preface to his book *The Formation of the Gospel Tradition* (1933), Form Criticism had attracted too little attention in Great Britain.[15] So, inevitably, the shock of Barthian theology was exacerbated rather than alleviated by the shock of the new approach to the composition of the Gospels.

The double impact of Neo-orthodoxy and Form Criticism undoubtedly gave English theology the stimulus it needed to make some sort of progress. On the other hand, it frightened as many scholars as it stimulated. The Jordan appeared to devout Anglo-Catholics and Evangelicals alike to be swollen with the waters of skepticism, and shrill cries could be heard calling for sandbags to defend the faith. It is instructive to study the reception accorded to the Bampton Lectures delivered by R. H. Lightfoot in 1934, and published in 1935 with the title *History and Interpretation in the Gospels*. Lightfoot had seen more clearly than most of his Oxford colleagues that source criticism of the Gospels had yielded most of the information it was capable of producing, and that the time had come to assess the value of the results achieved by the form-critical method. Accordingly he went to Germany in 1931 to discover for himself what light Bultmann and Dibelius had to throw upon the formation of the Gospels. What he learned there engrossed and excited him so much that he returned to England with a sense of vocation and mission to share it with his students. It was characteristic of the man that he had not the slightest desire to impress the academic world, and that he wrote his Bampton Lectures with extreme reluctance, solely for the benefit of the younger men. They were not outstanding lectures, but they served their purpose well, and in spite of the author's constant disavowal of originality they *were* original. They evaluated, more clearly than any other contemporary book, St. Mark's own contribution to the shaping of the Gospel message.

Some of the reviewers (e.g., B. T. D. Smith, of Cambridge[16]) damned Lightfoot's work with faint praise; others merely damned it. So far as I have been able to ascertain it did not receive a single favorable notice. Most of the critics fastened upon the famous last paragraph and claimed that it was more radically skeptical than anything that had come out of Germany. In this they not only displayed total failure to understand the meaning of Lightfoot's carefully chosen words, but also a rather insensitive attitude to his peculiarly religious method of exegesis, and finally their own ignorance of the Old Testament.

It will be recalled that Lightfoot's last lecture ended thus:

It seems, then, that the form of the earthly no less than of the heavenly Christ is, for the most part, hidden from us. For all the inestimable value of the Gospels, they yield us little more than a whisper of his voice; we have in them but the outskirts of his ways.

Only when we see him hereafter in his fullness shall we know him
also as he was on earth. And perhaps the more we ponder the matter,
the more clearly we shall understand the reason for it, and therefore
shall not wish it otherwise. For probably we are at present as little
prepared for the one as for the other.[17]

The Old Testament reference, which most of the reviewers
missed, was Job 26:14 (RV): "Lo, these are but the outskirts of
his ways: and how small a whisper do we hear of him! but the
thunder of his power who can understand?" And as Lightfoot
observed years later, Job

would have been even more grievously distressed than he already
was, had he thought that his words would be taken to imply that he
had practically no knowledge of his God. The last words of the
verse . . . show that the point of the passage lies in the contrast
between that comparatively small knowledge which in Job's view is
all that is at present available to man, and the boundless immensity
which is quite beyond his grasp.[18]

In these words written toward the end of his life, Lightfoot
gives us two clues to the meaning of the enigma with which he
concluded his lectures. First, the knowledge to which he refers
is the knowledge of *God.* Lightfoot's scholarship, like his religion, was theocentric and not Christocentric. Unlike the majority of his fellow Anglicans he would not, I think, have used
the prayer of St. Richard of Chichester, because his devotion was
toward God, and not toward the humanity of Christ. I make
no comment as to whether he was right or wrong in this devotional preference; I merely state what it was. For proof I need
only mention his inordinate admiration for the writings of Dean
Inge, especially those on mysticism. He even went so far as to
employ a press agency to send him cuttings from the newspapers
of every public utterance of the Dean, pasting them reverently
into an album which was discovered among his papers after his
death. Lightfoot's theocentric faith and mystical devotion enabled
him to follow his German "guides," as he called them, without

a trace of alarm or fear. His sole concern was the search for truth; he had no vested interest in preserving any kind of picture whatever of the human Jesus. To acknowledge that we know as little of the earthly as of the heavenly Christ was, in Lightfoot's view, to acknowledge the truth. He had no inkling at all that the admission of truth, as he saw it, might appear to critics (e.g., W. L. Knox) as "pathetic scepticism." [19]

The second of the two clues to a right understanding of Lightfoot's enigma lies in the contrast which he drew between the comparatively small knowledge which is at present available to man and the boundless immensity which is quite beyond his grasp. His course of lectures on the Fourth Gospel invariably contained an allusion to a quotation from Isaac Penington, which clearly illustrates what he meant: "All truth is shadow but the last, but every truth is substance in its own place, though it be but a shadow in another place; and every shadow is a true shadow, as every substance is a true substance." None of his contemporaries made as few claims for the current state of scholarship as Lightfoot; none spoke with greater modesty about his own achievements or those of others. This is not to say that he was skeptical of academic discoveries; in fact no one was warmer in his appreciation of them, and he would speak, almost with a sense of awe, of the work of C. H. Dodd and Ernst Lohmeyer whom he particularly admired. But they were *shadows* of a greater truth and he placed in them no *ultimate* confidence, "for he looked for the city which hath the foundations, whose builder and maker is God" (Heb. 11:10, RV).

W. L. Knox complained that Lightfoot did not contribute in any way to the solution of the difficulty of the relation of the "Jesus of History" to the "Christ of Experience." "For when all has been said and done, the synoptic Gospels do present us with the picture of a vivid and concrete personality, a figure we cannot profess to understand, but to which we can certainly render our allegiance, and, further, a figure which we cannot suppose

to have been constructed by the imagination of the first disciples." [20] Lightfoot's unpublished comment was: *"He* talks as if
the Gospel were a question of compiling the items of a radio
news bulletin, but *we* are concerned with the ultimate mysteries
of our faith." And that was his answer to Knox's complaint: he
would *not* contribute to the solution of the difficulty of the relation of the "Jesus of History" and the "Christ of Experience,"
because he saw that it was insoluble this side of the grave. Furthermore he had the wisdom and courage to say so.

Lightfoot's words were not heeded, partly because they
offended his readers' sense of devotion to the humanity of Christ,
and partly because, as Knox's words show only too clearly, Lib-
eralism was so entrenched in English theology that its exponents
could not bring themselves to give up altogether the quest of
the historical Jesus. But, if I am not mistaken, there was another
and more profound theological reason: their Christocentric faith
was not strong enough to endure the truth. As Professor G. W. H.
Lampe wrote in an article in the *Church Times* in 1962:

> To refuse to follow an enquiry beyond some boundary-line,
> determined by our preconceived ideas, is a denial of faith, a refusal
> to trust God, and an abandonment of the search for truth through
> fear of what we might find. Genuine faith does not need to take
> shelter from what too many Christians are apt to think of as the cold
> winds of criticism. On the contrary, it may find in the critical
> approach, alarmingly sceptical as this may seem at first sight, libera-
> tion from a bondage to the letter, different from that of which St.
> Paul wrote, but none the less genuine.[21]

Lightfoot's theocentric faith was massive; in spite of the fact that
his sensitive and generous nature was cruelly tortured by the
thoughtless and sometimes malicious criticism which he had to
suffer, he was not dismayed. It was, however, a childlike, mystical
faith, of a kind which is granted only to a few; the majority of
his readers would not have shared it. On the other hand, as
those who studied with Lightfoot immediately after the Second

World War can testify, there is no need of massive, or of mystical faith, to accept his main contentions with equanimity. We took them in our stride, and were not a little puzzled by our predecessors' failure of theological nerve.

Today the passage of time has lent perspective to the history of the interwar years, and brought the theological problems of that period into sharper focus. The failure of nerve is no longer quite so puzzling. Whatever faith theological students had in 1946, they had learned in the swelling of Jordan, in the engagement of war, in the uncertainty of life, in the shadow of the fear of death. It was a faith born of pessimism, of disillusionment, and of familiarity with suffering—small as a grain of mustard seed, and dark as the streets under a bombers' moon. But it was, in its small way, sturdy; not perhaps unshakable, but certainly unshockable, because it was always being challenged, and quite often shared, in the freer intercourse between friends effected by the war. It was the sort of faith the previous generation *could not have had* because it had not faced the reality of the question: "How wilt thou do in the swelling of Jordan?" Indeed it had scarcely begun to get its feet wet.

Now, in the '60's, the swelling of Jordan has become a jungle. (Jer. 12:5 is translated thus in the Revised Standard Version: "If in a safe land you fall down, how will you do in the jungle of Jordan?") The change from swelling to jungle is not altogether inappropriate. In the 1930's we were watching Germany in the process of rapid inflation into a great power, and we were beginning to experience the threat of an armed force greater than our own just across the North Sea. In the 1960's Russia's rapid growth is a thing of the past, and for some years we have been trying to counter the innumerable moves of an armed force greater than our own. In the 1930's we felt that the trouble was in one place, and built the pathetic Maginot Line to ward it off. In the 1960's there is trouble everywhere;

Cyprus, Cuba, Congo, South Africa, Indonesia, Vietnam, and so on. It is easier to count the peaceful nations than the troubled ones. If the Concise Oxford Dictionary is right in defining "jungle" as a "wild tangled mass," the world is a jungle indeed, and we do not know what to do or where to turn.

Theology is in a similar tangled state, and theologians appear to have created a jungle of their own. In 1946 the theology department of an Oxford bookshop consisted of a few shelves containing about 1,500 different volumes. Today the same department occupies a whole room at the back of the shop, and contains some 15,000 books. Most of this phenomenal increase seems to have taken place in the last ten years, and still shows no sign of abatement, in spite of the fact that the price of books has increased substantially.

The effect has been to distract the attention of scholars from their primary task of repairing the theological bastions of the Christian faith, so largely neglected in the interwar years. Lightfoot devoted his lifetime to the study of the second and fourth Gospels; he had a firm grasp of the literature on the subjects, and still had time in hand to devote himself to many other interests. He worked extremely hard—usually rising at 5 A.M.—but at the deliberate pace which serious academic study demands. His pupils are not so fortunate: they have to work faster and less thoroughly even to keep pace with the developments in a much smaller area of the total field than that to which Lightfoot devoted himself. At the same time they are obliged by postwar academic convention to publish more than he did. In consequence they are beginning to find it extremely difficult to see the wood—or should I say the jungle?—for the trees, and even harder to give their students an adequate map of the study of theology in its entirety.

Most of their energy and ingenuity has been spent in attempting to solve literary and historical questions, such as the relationship between the early Christian community and the

Qumran sect, or the nature of the text of the Bodmer papyrus. The strictly *theological* problems, such as demythologizing and the subsequent new quest of the historical Jesus, initiated by Rudolf Bultmann's pupils, Gunther Bornkamm in Germany and J. M. Robinson in the United States, have not until recently received so much attention. R. H. Fuller's recent book *The New Testament in Current Study,*[22] which is intended to be a brief résumé of progress since the war, looks more like an exposure of the distance between British and Continental scholarship. The question must therefore be raised whether British scholars *can* continue to confine themselves to literary and historical matters without doing disservice to the British Church, which is crying out for *theology* (whatever one may think of *Honest to God,* it is at least a symptom of that need). It suffered much in the '30's from the reluctance of its professors to come to grips with the vital theological problems raised by Neo-orthodoxy and Form Criticism. If it is to be preserved from a similar fate in the 1960's, there is urgent need for more thinking and writing of the kind advocated by the contributors to *Soundings.*[23]

However impenetrable the jungle may appear, there *is* a trail through it which is still open, though there is no time to be lost if we are to prevent it from vanishing in the undergrowth. Our first task is to rehabilitate the doctrine of God, in its proper place as the foundation of all theology. Paul Tillich has made this priority absolutely clear by devoting half of the first volume of his *Systematic Theology* to the subject. (Incidentally, it is interesting to note that whereas Tillich's *Systematic Theology* made its debut in England in 1953, the first significant British appreciation of it appeared no less than ten years later.[24]) But it is one thing to say that the doctrine of God should be rehabilitated, and quite another to say how it should be rehabilitated. My own view is that the direct and descriptive method of the Schoolmen no longer meets the case. Discussion of God's attributes or of the reasons for believing *that* he is do not satisfy the needs of those who want to know him *as* he is. What is required is less direct and more personal—a concrete and existential theology of prayer to substantiate both man's encounter with God and his communion with him, which are the two essentials of the Christian life. If we are to ride out the present theological storm, a reliable anchor is an indispensable necessity, and it seems to me that a new understanding of prayer is the only thing that can give us that anchorage. But, in view of the fact that the Christocentric devotion of the 1930's entirely failed to sustain theological progress, our new understanding of prayer must be ineluctably theocentric.

Our second task is to refuse to be seduced from the traditional priorities of Anglicanism by the special plea that Christology is the only starting point for theology. We must rather insist on a specifically theological examination of the presuppositions of New Testament Christology. For example, what are the theological repercussions of the new quest of the historical Jesus?

It will be recalled that, in Germany, Form Criticism begat such an extreme skepticism about what could be recovered of the actual words and works of Jesus that Bultmann gave up the quest entirely and concentrated instead upon the existential significance of the preaching of the early Church—the Kerygma. His pupils, however, have reacted against this extreme skepticism, and have taken a more moderate view. To quote an American commentator, Dr. Donald Rowlingson: "The Synoptic Gospels are evidence of the fact that some early Christians were concerned enough with reminiscences of Jesus to recall them and to preserve them. Recent studies also make abundantly clear that we can, with a fair degree of reasonableness, reconstruct many of the interests which prompted the appeal to the earthly Jesus." [25] Much the same is implied in these words of Dr. R. H. Fuller: "[there is a growing consensus among scholars] that the historical Jesus is both relevant and necessary to the Kerygma. Despite Bultmann's brave attempt to prove that for the Kerygma

only the bare facticity (the *Dass*) of Jesus matters, the trend
on all sides is to a recognition that the character and content
(the *Was* and the *Wie*) of his history are equally important." [26]
The *new* quest of the historical Jesus is a search for the character and content of his history.

It is important that Anglicans should join the quest, but it
is equally important that they should not see it as an enterprise
isolated from the rest of theology. In this respect they would be
well advised to refurbish a conviction which they have inherited
from the Greek Fathers. For the Fathers never studied the humanity of Christ as though it were an end in itself: on the contrary, it was for them not only the perfect human expression of
the image of God but also the ground of the Church and the
pledge of our ultimate participation in the divine nature (cf. II
Pet. 1:4). "In Christ, who is the perfection of the *imago Dei*
(Colossians 1:15), the diversity of natures is overcome by the
unity which establishes him as God in man, and man in God;
consequently, as St. Irenaeus saw, his becoming what we are
enables us to become what he is." [27]

In the writings of the Greek Fathers the doctrines of God,
Christ, and the Church were facets of one theological activity.
As the Archbishop of Canterbury has said, they "gave their deepest teaching about the Church without treating the Church as a
separate subject in itself. They did not expound the Church;
they expound Christ the Redeemer, and in such a way that the
Church is included in their exposition." [28] This tradition goes
back to the New Testament and finds its clearest expression in
Heb. 2:10 (RSV.): "For it was fitting that he, for whom and by
whom all things exist, in bringing many sons to glory, should
make the pioneer of their salvation perfect through suffering.
For he who sanctifies and those who are sanctified have all one
origin." That is why it is not enough that we should study the
humanity of Christ as an end in itself, and imperative that we
should do so in perspective, as part of the total activity of the-

ology. Nor should we be surprised if we discover that the humanity of Christ eludes us, or rather, leads us toward the consideration of the ultimate mystery of our redemption.

St. Mark recounts three prophecies by Jesus of the suffering of the Son of Man (8:31; 9:31; 10:33), and in each case the prophecies are immediately succeeded by further prophecies of the suffering and *kenosis* of the Church. I cannot escape the conclusion that he intended us to see the sufferings of the Son of Man as a prototype of the sufferings of the Church. This is surely what St. Paul meant when he said, "Have this mind in you, which was also in Christ Jesus" (Phil. 2:5, RV). In other words it is not a question of looking back at the historical Jesus in his detachment from the Church, but of looking forward *from* the sufferings of the earthly Christ, *through* the sufferings of the Church, *to* the ultimate glory of him through whom "God chose to reconcile the whole universe to himself" (Col. 1:20, NEB). This, at any rate, is what Lightfoot meant when he wrote, "Only when we see him hereafter in his fullness, shall we know him also as he was on earth"; and I believe those words are true.

9

Love and Justice Are the Same Thing

BY JOSEPH FLETCHER

The Question

The theme here—a perennial one in theological ethics—is the relation between love and justice. The thesis is that they are actually one and the same thing.

If I am right about this a great deal of time and thought have been wasted or imprisoned in a kind of conceptual revolving door, going round and round a "point of tension" which itself never gets anywhere. It is the purpose of this essay to show how the love-justice relation has been treated in representative modern moralists' work, and to explain why so much of it has been only "arrested development."

A few years ago Sammy Davis, Jr., a popular American entertainer, repudiated his Christian identity and became a Jew. "As I see it," he said, "the difference is that the Christian religion preaches love thy neighbor and the Jewish religion preaches justice, and I think justice is the big thing we need." [1] As a Negro who has suffered the injustice of discrimination he has our quick sympathy, but what about the inferred conception of love and justice in his words? The problem of conscience his revolt points at is obvious enough, bitterly obvious; but what of the *ethical understanding*, or misunderstanding, behind it?

The relation or tension between love and justice has been a central focus of Christian ethics and moral theology in all ages, but thus far without any result except confusion and foolishness. It does not arise in the same way in philosophical ethics and the cultural *mores*, nor do they get bogged down in conceptual worries and constant re-examination. This is because of two peculiarities in Christian ethics. (1) "Love" in the theological lexicon carries a nonromantic and nonaffectionate meaning. (2) The primary or pivotal imperative of the Christian *ethos* (possibly the only one) is the commandment to "love" one's neighbor. How then is this prime imperative of "love" to be related to the universal search for justice? Justice tends to be the core category in nontheological morality, love in theological morals. What is their true relation? And what *are* they?

The Problem

We might draw a parallel between the love-justice and the faith-works problems. Some theologies treat the latter as faith *versus* works, some as faith *or* works, some as faith *and* works, some as faith *is* works (i.e., simply put, "faith works"). In the same pattern we could find four different ways of relating love and justice: love *versus* justice, love *or* justice, love *and* justice, or love *is* justice. Are love and justice to be opposed to each other, served separately or alternatively, linked in coalition, or coalesced?

Bishop Anders Nygren's motif-research came close to making them an antithesis, by imbedding justice in *eros* (enlightened self-interest) and opposing *eros* to *agape* (disinterested love).[2] Denis de Rougemont has done the same thing.[3] But Father Martin D'Arcy has challenged them, arguing that the two "loves" (*agape* and *eros*) are not mutually exclusive, and hence justice is "on the side" of love.[4] Reinhold Niebuhr has in effect made them alternatives, regarding Christian love as impossible and only relative justice as within the range of possibility.[5] (Note, however, that Niebuhr's constructive ethics are somewhat equivocal through his use of "mutual love," meaning a relative, contingent, historically possible love.) In another way both Emil Brunner and William Temple have given love and justice separate and different relevances, holding that "love" is an imperative in interpersonal relations and "justice" in intergroup relations—Brunner speaking of "systems" and Temple of "organizations." [6] Brunner says that they are "radically different" although "akin." On the other hand, this separation of love and justice is challenged by Bishop Gustav Aulén in his *Church, Law and Society*.[7] G. Ernest Wright holds the same view, based on biblical studies: "These two conceptions simply cannot be separated because they are united in God." [8] And like Aulén and Wright, Canon Quick says that justice is "but one aspect or consequence of his [God's] all-creating and all-redeeming love," thus including the one in the other, yet not equating the two.[9]

Again love and justice are linked in coalition and mutual reinforcement by some—for example, by Paul Tillich who says that love "is the ground, the power, and the aim of justice" and, therefore, "Love without justice is a body without a backbone." [10] Indeed Tillich's treatment of love and justice, in relation to the factor of power, comes very close to the *fourth* approach to our problem, i.e., of coalescing or combining them into one. He actually says that love is "the ultimate principle of justice." [11] But this is not close enough. The fourth way of relating them has not actually been put forward in such straightforward terms, yet. This essay will do so. That is the only reason for writing it.

How, then, shall we set up the problem for careful scrutiny and analysis? There are, I suggest, three conceptual questions at stake here, and the way we answer them will determine how we relate love and justice. Put in their plainest fashion they are: (1) Are we to understand that "love" is emotional, a matter of feelings, while "justice" is volitional, a matter of "will" or determination? (2) Are we to regard "love" as personal and interpersonal, and "justice" as impersonal and "objective" (even putting a blindfold on it)? (3) Are we to think of "love" as particular and specific, and of "justice" as general and dispersed?

It seems evident that each of these three questions is inherent in the others, and therefore I propose a fourth coordinate question: Do not our answers to the second and third depend upon how we answer the first? This way of putting the question hints at the answer that I believe to be the right one: "Yes, all depends upon whether 'love' as such is an emotion or a volition. Let us firmly declare that it is a *volitional* category, not an emotional one. And therefore it is like 'justice'—in fact, the same thing."

However, if we are to attempt a fresh and independent construction of the question of the meaning of Christian "love" (*agape*) in relation to justice, we must go about it carefully, that is, with some care for the way others treat it. This can be done in a limited way which nevertheless reveals the variety of opinion available and the elements of equivocation which infect the whole discussion. Some of these equivocal elements may seem merely semantic, but we have learned not to say "merely" when we depart from the use of univocal terms in any serious discussion.

The Discussion

In a single, short book review recently I found the following typical conceptual confusions: "Love cannot be indifferent to justice"; "Justice is not complete without love"; "Love is a constituent element of justice"; and "We must act both justly and lovingly." Yet the reviewer's problem is not his alone. Let us look briefly at what representative moralists have said about the three questions we have framed.

1. *Are we to understand that "love" is emotional, a matter of feelings, while "justice" is volitional, a matter of "will" or determination?* A great majority answer in the affirmative, but it is a consensus only, not a universal agreement. For example, Nicolas Berdyaev treats Christian love as feeling.[12] Albert Schweitzer despaired of keeping any *agapeic* meaning in "love" and, faced with such interpretations as Berdyaev's, began using "reverence for life" instead, turning "love" over to friendship and romance as categories of mild or intense emotion.[13] Karl Barth, perhaps annoyed by Nygren's oversimple dichotomy of *eros* and *agape*, simply mixes the two.[14] Roman Catholic moral

and ascetical theology has traditionally treated "charity" as an appetite, along with justice and kindness and reverence, but their insistence on the supremacy of reason has tended to put "will" in charge as charity's primary quality. Thus Jacques Maritain and Bernard Haring have followed St. Thomas in regarding Christian love as *"friendship* with God and man"—making *agape* into *philia* in the manner of the Fourth Gospel.[15]

Most writers are more unambiguously insistent on the volitional nature of Christian love. According to Ethelbert Stauffer in the article on *agape* in Kittel's *Wörterbuch,* the Bible's use and distinction of three terms we translate as "love" was not consistently maintained, but generally its usage indicates: (*a*) *eran* as passionate desire, (*b*) *philein* as friendship feeling, and (*c*) *agapan* as more disinterested, without the intensity of *eran* or the warmth of *philein.* (*Agapan's* disinterestedness is none too clear in prebiblical Greek, but its prebiblical use is also infrequent.) Nevertheless, perhaps because of the suggestiveness of the Bible's different terms, constructive theologians are overwhelmingly in favor of assigning the "love" of the commandment (*agape*) a primarily nonemotional meaning. (They often say "primarily" because of their recognition that with the end of the old faculty psychology went any idea that the cognitive and conative or volitional functions of the human psyche can ever be entirely free of some admixture with affective or emotional dynamics.)

For example, C. H. Dodd says that *agape* "is not primarily an emotion or an affection; it is primarily an active determination of the will. That is why it can be commanded, as feelings cannot." [16] To illustrate, how could the promise to "love" in the marriage service be possible if "love" meant feeling? We cannot promise how we will *feel.* Hence Kant's conclusion about the Great Commandment, "it is only practical love [that is, benevolence or good will] that is meant in that pith of all laws." [17] Canon Herbert Waddams says even more forcefully in his *New Introduction to Moral Theology:* "It is extremely important to understand that love in the Christian sense is not primarily a matter of the emotions, although the emotions may be engaged. It is a matter of choice, choosing to submit to the will of God and to follow his path, and as a matter of choice its essential nature consists of an act of the will." [18] Almost all writers in the Anglican tradition have said the same, starting with Jeremy Taylor's assertion in his *Holy Living* (Chap. 4) that love is purpose rather than passion, that it is *not* liking. Another, more modern moral theologian, Bishop Kirk, reiterates the same point.[19] Still another, R. C. Mortimer, puts it this way: "The theological virtue of love is not primarily an emotion, its seat is in the will" and therefore "man is enabled to love God in the sense that by an act of the will he prefers God above everything else." [20]

Rudolf Bultmann is insistent. It is, he says, "now clear that *love does not mean an emotion* [his italics] . . . but a definite attitude of the will." And again, "Only if love is thought of as an emotion is it meaningless to command love: the *command* of love shows that love is understood as an attitude of the will." [21] C. E. B. Cranfield in the *Theological Wordbook of the Bible* says "*agape* refers to will rather than emotion, and often conveys the idea of showing love by action." [22] Millar Burrows, the biblical archeologist at Yale University, in his *Outline of Biblical Theology* explains: "What Jesus demands is not an emotion but an attitude of the will. . . . To love one's neighbor is not to feel affection for him but to wish and seek his good." [23] H. Richard Niebuhr and Waldo Beach put it very baldly: "To say love is a feeling or anything of that kind is really an unChristian conception of love." [24] And Reinhold Niebuhr agrees: "The ideal of love is first of all a commandment which appeals to the will." [25]

Martin Buber, a Jewish theologian biblically oriented, in his distinctive way says "the act of relation is not an emotion or a feeling. . . . Feelings accompany love, but they do not constitute it. . . . Hence love is not the enjoyment of a wonderful emotion, not even the ecstasy of a Tristan and Isolde, but the responsibility of an *I* for a *Thou*." [26] And further, he says that "love thy neighbor" certainly "does not mean loving feeling but loving action. One cannot command that one *feel* love for a person but only that one deal lovingly with him." [27]

Perhaps the most unpretentious way to understand *agape* is T. E. Jessop's, as a "certain bias or set" of the will! He held that "love as an emotion is more or less momentary or spasmodic; it is only love as an attitude that is continuous or lasting. The former is an effect of the latter, and only one of its effects." [28] As Tillich has pointed out, "One of the reasons for this misunderstanding of love is the identification of love with emotion. Love, like every human experience, of course includes an emotional element," but its essential nature is volition, choice, commitment, purpose.[29] It is discerning and critical, not sentimental. Its purpose is to satisfy the neighbor's need, not one's own, but the main thing about it is that *agape*-love precedes all desire of any kind. Its ethic is *Gesinnungsethik,* an attitudinal ethic, not emotional.

The point should now be clear. *Agape,* as distinguished from *philia* and *eros,* is the "love" of the commandment. And it is an attitude, a will-disposition, a matter of the conative—not the emotive. Only a perverse and stubborn sentimentalism will persist in treating it as feeling, although "feeling" is not to be deprecated or minimized as such, nor is it to be denied when it plays a part *in* the "bias" of *agape.* Yet the result is that we are to love the unlikable. Only in this way can we make sure we grasp the meaning of "Love your enemies."

In the same way, "justice" is conative, volitional, decision-oriented, purposive, dispositive—as *agape* is. As in the case of *agape,* we might of course "feel strongly" about justice too, but in their primary meaning both "love" and "justice" are volitional rather than emotional in the Christian interpretation. *They are not different*—love being a matter of "feeling" and "justice" a matter of "willing." They are not even merely alike. They are the same.

What of the second question?

2. *Are we to regard "love" as personal and interpersonal, and "justice" as impersonal and "objective" (even putting a blindfold on it)?* As we have seen, both Temple and Brunner found it possible to separate love and justice because they held the former to be relevant to persons only, reserving the latter as a norm or imperative for relations between "impersonal" or *group* entities. This is, of course, also the way that Martin Buber looks at the question in his influential *I and Thou,* and in *Between Man and Man.*[30] Yet we should take careful note that Buber has not put groups of related or even organized *I*'s and *Thou*'s into the world of *it*'s. Fraternities, associations, and even collectives (e.g., Buber's cherished *kibbutzim* in Israel) are still human and still personal.

Temple reasoned in *Christianity and Social Order* that there cannot be "love" between a labor union and a corporation or between one nation and another.[31] Yet, like Buber, Temple never actually characterized groups of persons as "impersonal." On the contrary, he defined a "person" as an individual who has been socialized by interaction with others, even using Buber's dialogic I-thou-it conception, although in complete ignorance, at the time, of the Continental Jewish philosopher.[32] Brunner, in maintaining that love belongs to the world of persons and justice to the world of "systems," meant that love is interpersonal while justice is social. Thus he claimed that in society the Christian has to "change his love into the current coin of justice." [33]

Brunner would, unlike Temple and Buber, finally and fundamentally divorce love and justice as entities. In *The Divine Imperative,* his *magnum opus* on Christian ethics, he flatly asserted that "love is never given to a collective body, even if this body were to consist of two people only; real community (*Gemeinschaft*) exists only between the 'I' and the single 'Thou.'" He added that once a third person enters the scene we are "no longer in the 'personal' sphere"—we are in "the realm of the 'orders' of human life." At the same time he acknowledges that such a "purely personal relation of love" to the neighbor is nonexistent, and that in fact we *"have* to deal with him as a member of the historical community." [34] To suppose, as Brunner does, that the Sermon on the Mount is addressed only to Robinson Crusoe and Friday is to make it more irrelevant and inviable than the most legalistic and pietistic expositions. And the human "person" he describes as a "single Thou" (he had no reference to God) is a sheer abstraction, a fiction of his theological imagination. Such a "person" is as fictitious as the "fictitious person" of the corporation in civil law; one is as unreal as the other.

On any calm, untendentious view, it is clear that we cannot separate the social from the personal. Each dimension of human existence is presupposed in the other. Therefore to speak of love as the "personal" and justice as the "social" is to unite the two terms.[35] But a more realistic view of things rejects both categories as separate entities. Personal and social are phases of being human, distinguishable but not separable, and the words "justice" and "love" are simply verbal signals that thinkers such as Brunner apply when they relate the norm of the "will of God" to the two phases. Justice is as "personal" as love, and "love" is as "social" as justice. We are commanded to love all of our neighbors whom we do not know interpersonally, even as we are to be just to the neighbor who is "nigh" or *here* in person. All men are *thou*'s, not *it*'s; they do not become *things* because they are too numerous or too distant. Therefore *agape* and justice require imagination and the ability to "care" for more people than we "know."

This leads us, by a logical entailment, into the third question.

3. *Are we to think of "love" as particular and specific, and of "justice" as general and dispersed?* If these three questions are as logically inherent in each other, coinherent, as I have suggested they are, then this one too must be answered "No"—as the first two were.

The one and the many, the particular and the general; these are age-old problems in the history of metaphysics. Parmenides'

and Plato's universals over against the "empirics" of theirs and
all times. The realists *versus* the nominalists. This is the archaic
antinomy of archaic philosophy. But none of it has ever helped
to settle any real issues, whether they are directly at stake in the
debate or only remotely involved. Certainly it brings no light to
the question under scrutiny here, probably because the attempt
to distinguish *and to separate* the particular from the general or
the one from the many is as artificial—as much a falsification
of reality—as the attempt to separate the personal from the social, as the attempt to separate love and justice themselves.

Since God's love is the source and "type" or prototype of
agape, it is of interest here to observe that even though there are
many references in the Old Testament to will-love or "good will"
(*aheb* or *chesed*), the love of God for human beings is ordinarily,
indeed consistently for collective subjects rather than particular
individuals. God's "love affair" is with the covenanted nation or
people or community, or even (as in the universal covenants)
with mankind, in "Adam" and Noah. For that matter, the "particular" covenants beginning with Abraham's in Gen., chapter
22, are not with individuals either, but with them and their seed
forever.

We all know the pitfalls of word study: how *chronos* can
do duty for *kairos, didachē* for *pistis,* and so forth. Biblical theology must take whole statements for the Bible's meaning, not
words alone. Yet even so, in the New Testament "love" is, like
justice, mainly understood as will or attitude and commitment.
The way they are practically equated in Luke 11:42 ("the justice and love of God") is revealing. In another episode the cen-
turion is said to "love our nation," and the term is *agape,* as with
God's love. There is no notion here like Kierkegaard's that love
is only for the "single one" and that a collectivity is a falsity.
Only in the Fourth Gospel is love often rendered by *philia* instead of *agape,* or mixed up practically interchangeably, as in the
famous instance of John 21:15-18. This being so it comes as no
surprise that the "love" of the Fourth Gospel is interpersonal, a

friendship relationship ("greater love than this has no man") along the lines of Brunner's thesis, or that the term "justice" is not present in that Gospel anywhere. This nonsocial or selective-exclusive meaning of "love" in the Fourth Gospel (for the "brother" or fellow believer but not for the "neighbor") is in contrast to the wider or more general reference of *agape* in the Synoptics and St. Paul.

There is a certain reasonableness back of the fear that the woods can blind us to the trees. William Blake's warning reminds us of it: "He who would do good to another must do it in minute particulars; general good is the plea of the scoundrel, the hypocrite, and flatterer." [36] Yet we are still faced with the hard fact that the tree is a part of the wood. In a forest fire we do not have to give each tree its own "name" in order to love it and do it justice by beating back the flames. It is too much and too simple to say, as Barth does, that "the State, the most impersonal because the most comprehensive of institutions, knows nothing of love." [37]

The problem of the relations of the particular to the general is like the problem of the personal and the social. The relationship is one of coinherence. To think or speak of the one is to think or speak of the other.

Justice is not alone in recognizing that there is more than one tree in the woods, more than one pebble on the beach. Love does too. This is why St. Augustine said that love calls for "more than good will, and can be done only by a high degree of thoughtfulness and prudence." [38] He meant that love in the same way as justice has to figure how to *distribute* its favors among many beneficiaries. The question of how to love justice is how to be just about love. *Love must be justice.* Granting the Aristotelian-Thomist-Brunnerian view that justice is giving to each man what is his due, how are we to calculate and "balance" love's benefits among so many claimants? This is precisely the problem of justice; the problem of love is no whit different. For love, *agape,* plays no favorites, exactly as "God is no respecter of persons" or "shows no partiality" (Acts 10:34; Rom. 2:11; Eph. 6:9, Col. 3:25, etc.).

Because we exist in community, love-justice is compelled to be calculating and distributive. The "neighbor" whom we are commanded to love is a generic *pleision*—neighbors in the plural. "Thou shalt love thy neighbors, all of them, as thyself." Only in this way can we avoid the oversimplifying, Tolstoyan notion that love wears blinders, never calculates, sees only the one-to-one *immediate* neighbor who is to be loved, one at a time.[39] To embrace such a notion, as so many have, is to fail to see that love is justice, justice love. For justice is no respecter of persons, shows no partiality, loves all alike, exactly as "God is no respecter of persons," and chooses no friends (Acts 10:34; Rom. 2:11; Eph. 6:9; Col. 3:25). Behind such a phrase as "love is the soul of justice," getting close to the simple truth, is a recognition that love is the effective principle of justice; and justice is love balancing interests and claims, calculating, "sorting its mix" (in the language of the game-theory analysts). The upshot of all this is that "love" and "justice" are to be related not as one plus one, which equals two, but as one times one—which equals only *one*.

The Solution

There are at least three summary things to be said now, which are supported by the thesis we have been developing.

The *first* thing is that "love" and "justice" equally are volitional, when Christianly understood—even though susceptible often of an emotional admixture. Both are, at the same time, at once personal and impersonal. They are also, both of them, particular and general. What may be said properly of either of them applies to the other.

The *second* thing is that "love" and "justice," as classical terms with a long and noble history in Christian moral theology, mean exactly what is meant in philosophical ethics by "goodness" or "the good." As with goodness, so with love and justice, we must never forget that such terms or epithets are predicates, not properties. "Love" and "justice" are something that *happens,* not something that is. Each is extrinsic and contingent in any action or relationship, not intrinsic or given. The theological observation is that only the love of God, who *is* love, is a property. It follows, therefore, that the love-justice which God commands and requires of men may only be *predicated,* if and when they are obedient—but only if and when. *Agape* or neighbor-love is not something we have or give. It is something we do or do not do. And so with justice.

All serious English ethical analysis since G. E. Moore's *Principia Ethica* at the turn of the century has seen for what it is (a phantasm) any reification or objectification of "good" or of value concepts. Moore's "naturalistic fallacy" has always undermined and misdirected those who attempt to "thing-ify" love and justice. I would go farther. I would have to agree with Stephen Toulmin's brilliant demonstration that such notions, whether taken as "values" or "imperatives," are not even "non-natural" or "unanalysable" properties.[40] They just are not properties at all, only predicates, except for God himself—since as Jesus pointed out, "With men this is impossible, but with God all things are possible" (Matt. 23:26). This is why H. Richard Niebuhr could insist that "Jesus never commanded love for its own sake." [41] Love that pretends to *be* something in and of itself is a self-contradiction. It is on this elemental level of ethical theory that we have to oppose Tillich's attempt in *Love, Power and Justice* to give love and justice an ontological status, even though he pleases us by refusing to separate them or to give one a higher "value" than the other.

The *third* thing is that all of this means, in the simplest and most direct language, that love and justice are one and the same thing. Hence the persistence in the past of such maxims as "justice is the soul of love" and "love is the soul of justice." What we call love is justice, as justice is love. Neither is a phase nor a partner nor a prerequisite nor a consequence of the other. They are coeval, coterminous.

Their complete identity may be recognized in this way—by seeing how they both "go out" to their many neighbors on all hands, responsibly ignoring Tolstoy's notion (his anarchist notion) that love cannot count and knows no future, and trying instead to balance their favors among them all with a realistic eye to consequences. Then it can be recognized. Love is justice, love is just. Justice is loving—using its head, calculating its duties, sharing its obligations, seeking the good of as many neighbors as possible.

The idea of Reinhold Niebuhr, that love and justice are different, love being "higher" and justice more "possible," has its counterpart in Roman Catholic moral theology. There it has actually been held that love and justice can come into conflict—in which case love may be denied in order to do justice.[42] Actually, when the love-ethic removes the blinders which narrow its field of vision to one neighbor at a time, it forms a coalition with the utilitarian principle of "the greatest good of the greatest number." In this partnership or "front" the *procedural* principle of utilitarianism ("the greatest number") and the normative principle of the Commandment ("love your neighbor") result in "the greatest amount of *agape* for the greatest number of neighbors possible." That is justice. And even if we define justice as "paying what is due" (a rather static notion), the *Christian* understanding of "what is due" to our neighbor is "all the love possible." Love and justice are the same.

The Conclusion

All of this is a serious thesis about a serious question in theological ethics. Paul Tillich has called upon the Christian Church to "demonstrate in teaching, preaching, and liturgy the unconditional demand of justice in the very nature of *agape*." [43] Justice is the very nature of Christian love, and love of justice.

A practical difficulty is the semantic confusion. In a worldwide usage the word "love" has a romantic connotation. Qualifying "love" with "Christian" does not eliminate the sentimental suggestion. (Even in Japan, when *agape* is translated as *ai* the same confusion and red herring ensues as in English with "love.") Tillich says, "I believe it would be salutary if the word 'love' in the sense of *agape* could be avoided for a long time, and the word *agape* introduced into modern language." [44] *Agape* at least comes to people as a new word, so that they ask, "What's that?" and thus hear better what is meant than if, by misconstruing, they respond with, "Oh!"

But I have another recommendation. *The best practice is never to use the word "love" in Christian ethical discourse.* Every time we think "love" we should *say* "justice." For justice has not been hopelessly sentimentalized, or romanticized, or individualized. Not only *is* it Christian love but, as communication, it *says* it. It says what the biblical *agape* means. If we are to have one ethical *logion*, as St. Paul put it in Gal. 5:14, then let it be *justice*. (And it is possible, at least, that Paul was leaning in the same direction by his frequent use of *dikaiosunē*—that justice or righteousness which is the mark of the man in Christ, who is the Man for *all* others.)

Jeremy Taylor, that Anglican bishop and casuist who spoke as much for the Puritans as for the high churchmen of the Caroline seventeenth century, said flatly in *Ductor Dubitantium*: "God cannot do an unjust thing, because whatever he wills or does is therefore just, because he wills and does it, his will being the measure of justice." [45] Exactly so. Love is *his* being, justice is what he wills for *our* doing. Our Christian business is not to try to be God, but to do God's will—that is, justice.

Perhaps because I coalesce love and justice in this direct way I shall be accused of being too Old Testamentish. If so I don't mind. I am no crypto-Marcionite. If we take seriously the prophetic genius of the Bible we should have no trouble seeing the *henōsis* of love and justice or using "justice" as its name.

10

Music and Belief—Two Questions

BY WILLIAM H. RALSTON

Is there any way to distinguish between sacred music and secular music? Is it possible for music to serve an explicitly theological function and retain its integrity as music? On the other hand, does not the best liturgical music overpower the very words it is meant to serve, attracting by itself and to itself the numinous and passionate response of the worshiper? Is not music completely nontheological and, even more radically, areligious? Can music really be baptized for the Church? Or is it not, like mysticism, a universal phenomenon, the practical significance of which is always elusive of explanation, and completely destructive of all dogmatic claims to control or confine it?

In a now-famous essay[1] Karl Barth has declared his "faith in Mozart," in Mozart alone among all makers of music. "I must confess: there is he and nobody else." Not only does Barth's faith in Mozart provide a unique category for this composer among all others, it also puts Mozart first in Barth's affections before all theologians, before even his own *Dogmatik*. ". . . I have listened to Mozart's music the first thing in the morning for years and years. Only after this . . . have I given attention to my *Dogmatik*. I must further confess: If I ever go to heaven I would first of all inquire about Mozart. . . ." And Barth concludes an imaginary "Letter of Thanks to Mozart" with this: "I have only a hazy feeling about the music played there where you now dwell. I once formulated my surmise about that as follows: whether the angels play only Bach in praising God I am not quite sure; I am sure, however, that *en famille* they play

144

Mozart and that then also God the Lord is especially delighted to listen to them. Well, this *alternative* may be wrong. Besides, you know that better than I do, anyhow. I mention this only in order to hint metaphorically at my meaning."

In the whole of Barth's works there is nothing more mysterious or more moving than this. It is enough to change the entire perspective in which his theology may be read. Because Barth is who he is and what he is, it seems to me imperative to try to comprehend the meaning of his "faith in Mozart." I think by this effort of comprehension we will secure a right direction toward the answer to the question put at the beginning.

It certainly would be odd to discover a nontheological factor at work in the thought of this immensely theological man, and in fact Barth has a theological reason for his faith. It is because Mozart has no discoverable *Dogmatik* of his own that Barth can believe in him. "Mozart's music, in contrast to that of Bach, has no message, and contrary to that of Beethoven, involves no personal confession. His music does not give rules, even less does it reveal the composer himself. . . . Mozart does not wish to say anything at all; he just sings and sounds." "It is as if a small part of the universe is singing."

Barth does not think that Mozart's music is without meaning, in the sense that it is devoid of significant content. For him it is uniquely full of meaning, but the music itself is the meaning, and cannot be commented upon or explained by circumstances external to itself. Then how can Barth write an essay about it, or have faith in it? "Mozart always had something to say, and said it as player and composer. However, you should not complicate or mar the impression of his works by burdening them with doctrines or ideologies which you think one has discovered, but which in reality have been read into them. There is no 'moral of the story' in Mozart's works, neither a gross nor a sublime one." "The fact is that, whether we like it or not . . . , neither the nature surrounding him nor the history, literature, philosophy or politics of his time touched him directly or in a concrete sense. Nor was he moved to represent or proclaim any decisions or dogmas."

This does not and could not mean for Barth the kind of retreat into aesthetic inaccessibility by which one attempts to isolate Art in all its forms from reasonable discourse, and provide for it a kind of invulnerability and immunity from humane interpretation. For Barth, Mozart's music is tremendously human, and of the very substance of what we mean by "personal." He does retreat from the attempt to explain the music in terms of realities or experiences other than or outside itself; but at the same time there is in his essay a retreat *into* the very depths from which both Mozart's music and Barth's own theology come. In the center of Mozart's music what happens is ". . . a splendid annulment of balance, a *turn* in the strength of which the light rises and the shadow winks but does not disappear; happiness outdistances sorrow without extinguishing it and the 'Yes' rings stronger than the still-existing 'No.' . . . He always executed that comforting turn which is priceless for everyone who hears it. That seems to me, as far as it can be explained at all, to be the secret of his *freedom* and thereby the nucleus of his singular quality. . . ."

Someone may object that this uses nonmusical references in order to explain what Barth has declared to be significant simply because it is music, music which only sings and sounds. It is the same kind of objection that is sometimes brought against his theology. Barth could and probably would say that in speaking of Mozart he "spake as a fool," but also that he might not remain silent about so great and so important a mystery. There is a world of difference between his type of "explanation," which implicitly denies its own adequacy as explanation even as it explains, and the elaborate political or sociological or psychological or theological structures in terms of which music is often made to speak. Although Barth's explanation is a dark one, there is light enough, and we are in a different world altogether from the obscurantism of professional aesthetes. Unless we are to remain completely dumb about music, and indeed about any form of human art whatever, we must use language, and language is always in one way or another technical language. Barth writes about Mozart's music as a theologian, and his language takes its color and derives its deepest rational significance and emotional resonance from that fact. Perhaps only someone thoroughly committed to theology can take Barth's essay in its full range of articulate meaning, but the basic sense of it is accessible to any humanely educated person. It is not only as one committed to theology that I would call Barth's essay the finest and most important single piece of musical criticism in existence. Nothing is forced on the music. Instead the reader is taken into the heart of it by a whole series of attributes, each stated in such a way that it carries its own limitation as an explanation along with it. The end is illumination.

For the question posed at the beginning of this essay, the striking thing about Barth's belief in Mozart is the absence of any explicit theological content. Indeed it is *because* Mozart is without any formal theological meaning that Barth can believe in him and in no other. Mozart's music is not theologically neutral, for that is an impossible thing, but it is never dogmatic and never explicit. Mozart "does *not* want to proclaim the praise of God, either. However, he does just that. . . ." Barth asks us, and himself as well: "How is it possible that I, an evangelical Christian and theologian, can so proclaim Mozart? How could I do this even though he was such a Catholic and even a Freemason and besides through and through nothing else than just a musician? . . . May I ask all . . . who perhaps shake their heads in astonishment and alarm, to be momentarily contented with the general reference to the fact that the New Testament speaks not only about the kingdom of heaven, but also of the *parables* of the kingdom of heaven?"

Mozart's music is a parable of the kingdom and, as such, a work of the Word of God. But it has no "message" and speaks no "doctrine," nor can we discover from the music anything about Mozart which is able to be conceptualized as a message or a doctrine. His music is a dark speech in reference to everything except the personal center of his own being, which cannot be subjected to formulation, but which, for Barth at least, mediates through the music made by the person something of the way reality ultimately is. We have already noted how Barth distinguishes the music of Mozart in this respect from that of all other composers. Bach has a message, and Beethoven a confession to give us; and we are grateful to Schweitzer for helping us receive Bach's message, to Sullivan and Burnet James for making it possible for us to hear Beethoven's confession, with all the moral problems that involves—but Barth is not much interested in either of these things. In a recorded interview not long ago he reaffirmed his faith in Mozart, saying something like this: I listen only to Mozart. Not Beethoven. No. Never Beethoven. Beethoven tells me about himself. Mozart only sings and plays.

A most formidable problem emerges from this. It seems that Mozart's music becomes theologically significant precisely in that it does not involve theology as such. The music is completely free to be itself. It is autonomous. Its value is that it has not been adjusted, nor has it been made instrumental to any other reality. This approach to the problem (or is it a mystery?) of the relation of music to other forms of knowledge, whether physical or psychological or even theological, is very powerful. It means that music—or painting or poetry or any science—is free to obey the laws of its own nature and develop along its own lines. There is no coercion of music from any foreign sphere of knowledge, no intrusion of any other than musical experience.

Thus Norman Pittenger, writing of hearing a performance of the Fourth Symphony of Brahms, can say: "I sat enthralled by the beauty of the performance. . . . There was a sheer joy in it, yet also the depth of human experience and sorrow. The next day I happened to return in memory to the evening in Carnegie Hall, and suddenly I said to myself, 'That was God speaking to us, and we did not recognize Him.' But a moment later I realized that to have thought specifically religious thoughts, to have tried to turn the whole aesthetic experience into a religious one, would have destroyed the value of it, robbed it of its autonomous dignity and beauty. Yet the fact that I can and do relate that music to God, and find whispered intimations of Him there, that the music and my religious faith fit into a pattern of which the very heart and center is belief in and communion with God, makes the whole experience a richer and deeper thing, and life in all its complexity as in all its simplicity becomes more meaningful for me." Though there should be no intrusion of dogmatic religion into this very different kind of experience, still, as Pittenger goes on to say, "not to be able to relate (this) *ultimately* to God, nor to know that *in the religious moment* it finds its place and receives heightened significance in retrospection, would be to make it less than it might be—would, indeed, ruin it in yet another sense."

The same point is made, though indirectly, in Samuel Antek's moving and wonderfully illuminating account of playing with Toscanini. In attempting to assess the difference between Toscanini and all other conductors, and so give some explanation of the unique quality of the musical performances conducted by him Antek writes: "[Toscanini] conducted the music, not the orchestra." "The image he created not only became clear to us, but peculiarly and convincingly our own. We did not feel like puppets being made or told to do something; we felt completely identified with what was going on. Music was no longer abstract notes; it was the symbol of our most moving, deep-felt experience." [2]

The problem is put when this profoundly theological appreciation of the freedom of music is contrasted with what is

almost a dogma for music that is to be utilized in the service of
the Church. Such music in no sense may exist for itself. It exists
rather "to enhance the worship of the Church, through the
beauty of sound, by the reinforcement of the words . . . or by
the establishment of a mood or atmosphere for the service." These
words from the 1961 Report of the Joint Commission on Church
Music of the Episcopal Church restate a venerable Catholic opinion[3] that music in church is the "handmaid of religion" and that
"all true religious music [is] but exalted prayer." At the same
time, since nothing may or should be used for the glory of God
in the worship of the Church save the very best, whether of
music or architecture or vesture, it follows that the music which
serves the uses of the Church must be not only adequate to the
needs of the services, but also good in itself as music, and comparable in excellence with music produced simply as music, without additional motive.

Yet the nature of this music which the Church seeks for her
own use is severely prescribed—"All music, whether instrumental
or vocal, which contains anything lascivious or impure, must be
entirely kept out of Churches." It is very hard to detect impurity
in music, but the usual Catholic position is that "pure" music
for the Church is vocal music, without instrumental accompani-
ment. Plain chant is the ideal of religious music considered this
way. The human voice is "the immediate vehicle of the sacred
Word," and the introduction of instruments, even the organ, is
a definite compromise in the direction of theatricalism. This,
along with sentimentalism and virtuosity, is the chief tempta-
tion of music written for the Church, and when yielded to becomes a sin against worship in the name of sound. Mozart is
the great example. His so-called secular music, both instrumental
and vocal, is universally held to be of the very essence of music
itself, as purely and simply *music* as can be. But his music for
liturgical purposes, with the exception of a few isolated mo-

ments, is rejected on the grounds of both its virtuosity and its theatricality.

What often happens when music is composed to order for the Church is that music becomes not a handmaid but a bond-servant, obediently supplying what is considered by ecclesiastical authority an appropriate sound for this or that portion of the Church's worship. It is well to remind ourselves that those very compositions which we now regard as the masterworks of music for the Church, the polyphonic marvels of Josquin des Pres, di Lasso, Palestrina, and many others, were viewed either with great suspicion or with open hostility when they were new, and were frequently condemned precisely for virtuosity and theatri-cality. Palestrina's victory over the Fathers of Trent, in persuad-ing them to accept polyphony against their collective puritan will, is a delightful re-enactment of the Orpheus story in a Chris-tian context. Religion in any of its structural forms, whether as dogmatic theology or as ecclesiastical authority, has always found it very difficult, and sometimes impossible, to accept the freedom of music. The exclusion of certain musical modes from the Re-public is a notorious Platonic puritanism, and formal religion has always tended either to condemn some music outright or to re-strict it so severely that it virtually ceases to function as an inde-pendent activity of the spirit. H. L. Mencken shows this type of discrimination among musical proprieties, with its peculiar li-ability to absurdity, precisely for what it is: ". . . The delusion seems to persist that jazz is highly aphrodisiacal. I never encoun-ter a sermon on the subject without finding it full of dark warn-ings to parents, urging them to keep their nubile daughters out of the jazz palaces on the ground that the voluptuous music will inflame their passions and so make them easy prey to bond sales-men, musicians and other such carnal fellows. All this seems to me to be nonsense. . . . The truth is that jazz is probably the least voluptuous variety of music commonly heard in Christen-

dom. There are plenty of Methodist hymns that are ten times
as aphrodisiacal, and the fact is proved by the scandals that follow every camp-meeting. In most parts of the United States, indeed, the Methodists have begun to abandon camp-meetings as
subversive of morality. Where they still flourish it is not unusual
for even the rev. clergy to be taken in Byzantine practices. But
so-called good music is yet worse than the Methodist hymns." [4]
And Mencken goes on to illustrate the point with *Tristan und
Isolde, Parsifal,* and *La Boheme!*

The issue becomes very sharp indeed. In theory the Church
wants only the best music, but in practice it wants only useful
music, music which will serve without protest the immediate
needs of the Church's service. The official ideal of Church music
would seem to be a music which serves in silence.

All this does suggest a possible solution to the problem in a
distinction which has been implied but not so far stated—a distinction between liturgical music and "religious" music. ". . .
We carefully distinguish between simply religious music—be it
never so beautiful, artistic, and conducive to private devotion—
and that kind of music which the Church requires for her
services." [5] This is surely a most important distinction, but it
does not in any way solve the problem. It simply covers it. For
it remains unclear in just what sense good *liturgical* music can be
distinguished from plain good music. It certainly *is* clear to any-
one with ears that most so-called liturgical music, the actual music
used by the Church in the majority of her services, is incalculably
inferior as music to most so-called secular music, and to most
nonliturgical "religious" music as well. I think this explains the
nostalgia for plain chant, the simplest and best of all forms of liturgical music. Only here is there a music, both beautiful and strong
in itself, which perfectly accommodates the words whose meaning it serves to enhance. But even here one must be content
with the early, simple chants (whose innate vigor is often con-
cealed by the effete manner of performance), not the florid

elaborations of the Middle Ages. Is it not hard to reduce significant good music for the Church—that is, properly *liturgical*
music—to the primitive stage of only one particular form? Surely
this is a most sectarian exegesis of the history of Church music.

Although the distinction between liturgical music—service
music for the Church—and religious music with no specific
liturgical commitment is a pragmatically justifiable one, it avoids
the main point and begs the most important question: Can music
in fact be made a vehicle for something which in itself is nonmusical, even if that something is the Word of God, or the words
of the Church of God, without being destroyed as music? By
imposing the requirements of liturgical use do you not almost
ensure the production of inferior, even bad music in the very
place where only the best should be admitted? It ought to be
a dreadful shock to any Christian to hear Beethoven's *Missa
Solemnis* or the *Requiem* of Verdi in a concert hall, yet we are
constantly being assured that this is their only suitable milieu,
that they are completely nonliturgical, and are correctly banished
from liturgical use precisely because they are (and they are!)
theatrical and virtuosic in conception and execution. But what
strictly liturgical music of the same period is within light-years of
either of them *as music?*

Mozart's liturgical music (or is it just religious? or is it
neither liturgical nor religious?) remains the most difficult case.
It has seemed to most commentators to be a complete seculariza-
tion of music for the Church, an absolute antithesis to the ideals
held up for liturgical music. Yet it is in relation to just this music
that Barth makes his most profound, and profoundly mysterious,
remarks. "[Mozart's church music] has been repeatedly called
worldly or even operatic. . . . Only this much is true: his work
in this field has never measured up to the known dogma that the
sound (*Ton*) must only serve, only interpret the word. But is
this the only possible dogma for church music? . . . If I hear
correctly, his sound in his church and other music is a free mirror

of the word given to him. The sound is inspired by the word, it
accompanies and plays around it. The sound corresponds to the
word; and this means indeed that the sound gets and preserves its
own life in relation to the word. . . . [Mozart] hears and re-
peats the word here and there in its own content and character,
yet he adds music, his own music, here and there—a creature of
his own, bound through the word but sovereign in spite of its
bond." And Barth sums up all this in a remarkable sentence, one
as significant for our understanding of his own theology as for
the problem of the relation of the sacred and the secular in
music: ". . . Mozart's church music has been heard and repro-
duced from a point where God and the world are not identical
but from which church and world (these two not confoundable
or exchangeable) are recognizable and recognized in their relative difference but at the same time in their ultimate homogeneous-
ness, both in the relation of God to them and in their relation to
God."

    If it is not too much like mixing oil and water to use Til-
lich to help interpret Barth, I would say that Barth is directing
us toward a criterion for religious and liturgical music which,
in Tillich's language, we have learned to call the capacity of
created things for revealing the depth of reality at the same moment in which they are completely themselves. There is, if you
will, a fundamental bond of being which obtains for music as
well as anything else; an ontological holding together of everything, in which music participates. There can be no ultimate
difference between good secular music and good sacred music,
nor can there be music that supplies a reasonable service to the
liturgy that is not also good music, unless both liturgy and music
would be ruined together. To say that something which is not
good music absolutely is, however, good liturgical music is nonsense. Nor can there be any segregation of a liturgical as opposed
to a merely religious style. Palestrina could charm Trent only
by his polyphony. This was the characteristic sound of his own

music *as* music. Mozart's sound is utterly different, but is it not equally appropriate? Why should Stravinsky not compose a *Lamentations* using serial technique? It is the sound of *his* music and, along with Palestrina and Mozart, a parable of the kingdom. This recognition of depth, a way of saying that our eyes and ears have been opened, is the reason why theology, unlike all other "ologies," can supply a basis for music which does not enslave music but instead provides the very conditions for its freedom. The moment that theology tries to dictate the *form* of this freedom, then the freedom is lost. Stravinsky says: "Whether or not the Church was the wisest patron—though I think it was; we commit fewer musical sins in church—it was rich in musical forms. . . . I say simply that, without the Church, 'left to our own devices,' we are poorer by many musical forms." [6] This is a musical and not a theological judgment, just as Barth's essay is a theological and not directly a musical one. But as Barth opens for us the depth of Mozart's music, so Stravinsky helps us to see the same problem of the relation of sacred and secular in music from another angle, that of the musician himself.

We are fortunate that Stravinsky should be so articulate about the foundations of his music. It is something that almost all great composers are either silent about or find themselves unable to express clearly in words.

I don't know what Barth thinks of Stravinsky's music. For myself I agree with the judgment that his works which set sacred texts are "the strongest challenge in two hundred years to the decline of the Church as a musical institution." Stravinsky has written an explicitly liturgical Mass, and a considerable body of what we must still (although misleadingly) call "religious music." What this music means to himself Stravinsky has nobly said: "The Church knew what the Psalmist knew: music praises God. Music is as well or better able to praise Him than the building of the church and all its decoration. It is the Church's greatest ornament. Glory, glory, glory. . . ." Stravinsky defines the basic

purpose of music: "to reveal itself as a form of communion—
with our fellow-man and with the Supreme Being." [7] For him
music is a form of communion with and participation in God.
His own lovely *Symphony in C,* which is simply music, was
written, by the composer's own testimony, "to the glory of God."
So also his *Symphony of Psalms.* Evidently there is no distinction
of persons in Stravinsky's musical commonwealth. His statements
make chaos of the placid utilitarianism of our commissions and
encyclopedias.

Music praises God. It praises him whether it does so through
liturgical action or without any other reference whatever. There
is no specifically religious music. Even more, there is no distinctively Christian music. The practical day-to-day needs of the
Church for music in its services, legitimate and proper as these
needs are, can never be sufficient grounds for accepting in any
but the most embarrassed sense music for the Church which is
not, judged simply as music, the best music. One of the most
perceptive and musical people I know said once: "For a composer
to write music is to obey God; for him to try to write Christian
music is to play God."

Music praises God by being its own best self. But, more
deeply, when it can be its own best self in right relation to that
other and more specific realm of grace wherein even music can
serve without coercion, then there is the kind of sacramental rais-
ing of music in which it becomes able, as Stravinsky says, "to
represent Paradise and become 'the bride of the Cosmos.' "

Barth declares his faith only in Mozart. Some others of us
believe in Stravinsky as well, and in Bach and Verdi, even in
Beethoven, with his self-preoccupation and self-dramatization.
And yet, just here, when the problem seems to be unfolding itself
at last, another consideration arises. When Stravinsky was asked
whether one must himself be a believer in order to compose in
the liturgical forms of the Church, he replied: "Certainly, and
not merely a believer in 'symbolic figures,' but in the Person of

the Lord, the Person of the Devil, and the Miracles of the Church." No revelation of Barth's faith in Mozart could be more astonishing than this confession, in the mid-twentieth century, by our *princeps musicae*.

For if a specific content of faith is the condition of integrity in composing in liturgical forms, have we not compromised the autonomy and universality of music by making it an instrument of personal confession? The result would be that the musical judgment must somehow wait upon doctrinal issues. And how then could choice be made between the *Requiem* of the skeptical, agnostic Verdi, and the *Beatitudes* of the devout and saintly Franck? It is not the religion but the music of the two men which is decisive. It is not impossible to hear more Christianity in Verdi's *Kyrie* than in the whole of Franck's music taken together. And the final irony is that Stravinsky, the musician, must believe specifically in order to compose his music in certain forms, whereas Barth, the theologian, can listen to only one man's music because the forms of that music give no evidence of any specific belief at all. Here is yet another mystery, and another question.

W. Norman Pittenger—A Bibliography: 1931-1964

ASSEMBLED BY DURSTAN R MCDONALD

I. BOOKS

Approach to Christianity. New York: Morehouse-Gorham, 1939; and London: Geoffrey Bles (Centenary Press), 1939.

This Holy Fellowship: The Ancient Faith in the Modern Parish. With E. R. Hardy, Jr. New York: Morehouse-Gorham, 1939.

Christ and Christian Faith: Some Presuppositions and Implications of the Incarnation. New York: The Round Table Press, 1941.

Christian Faith and Worship. New York: Morehouse-Gorham, 1942.

The Christian Way in a Modern World. Louisville, Ky.: The Cloister Press, 1944.

Stewards of the Mysteries of Christ. Louisville, Ky.: The Cloister Press, 1945.

His Body the Church. The Bohlen Lectures for 1945. New York: Morehouse-Gorham, 1946.

Living Faith for Living Men: Simple Studies in Great Subjects for Lay People. Louisville, Ky.: The Cloister Press, 1946.

What Does the Episcopal Church Stand For? Some Answers for Visitors and Inquirers. New York: Morehouse-Gorham, 1946.

Sacraments, Signs and Symbols. With Essays on Related Topics. Chicago: Wilcox and Follett, 1949.

Historic Faith and a Changing World. New York: Oxford University Press, 1950.

Christian Sacrifice: A Study of the Eucharist in the Life of the Christian Church. New York: Oxford University Press, 1951.

The Faith of the Church. With James A. Pike. New York: The Seabury Press, 1951.

The Principles and Practice of Christian Faith. London: S.C.M. Press, 1951.

Christ in the Haunted Wood: The Christian Foundation for the Good Life. New York: The Seabury Press, 1953; and Toronto: Oxford University Press, 1953.

Christian Affirmations. New York: Morehouse-Gorham, 1954; and London: The Holborn Publishing and Distributing Co., 1954.

The Christian View of Sexual Behaviour: A Reaction to the Kinsey Report. New York: The Seabury Press, 1954; and Toronto: Oxford University Press, 1954.

What Is the Priesthood? A Book on Vocation. With J. V. Butler. New York: Morehouse-Gorham, 1954.

J. F. Bethune-Baker, *The Faith of the Apostles' Creed.* Edited by W. Norman Pittenger. New York: The Seabury Press, 1955; and Toronto: Oxford University Press, 1955.

Theology and Reality: Essays in Restatement. New York: The Seabury Press, 1955; and Toronto: Oxford University Press, 1955.

J. F. Bethune-Baker, *Early Traditions about Jesus.* Edited by W. Norman Pittenger. New York: The Seabury Press, 1956.

Rethinking the Christian Message. New York: The Seabury Press, 1956.

Tomorrow's Faith Today. Essays on Rethinking the Christian Message Toward a New Modernism. New York: Exposition Press, 1956.

The Church, the Ministry, and Reunion. New York: The Seabury Press, 1957; and Toronto: Oxford University Press, 1957.

The Episcopalian Way of Life. Englewood Cliffs, N.J.: Prentice-Hall, Inc., 1957; and London: Bailey Brothers and Swinfen, 1957.

The Liberal Spirit in Religion. Faculty Papers, Series IV. Edited, with E. G. Ballard. New York: The National Council of the Protestant Episcopal Church, 1957.

W. P. DuBose, *Unity in the Faith.* Edited by W. Norman Pittenger. New York: The Seabury Press, 1957; and Toronto: Oxford University Press, 1957.

M. L. Yates, *God in Us: The Theory and Practice of Christian Devotion.* Edited, with W. H. Ralston. New York: The Seabury Press, 1959; Toronto: Oxford University Press, 1959; and London: S.P.C.K., 1959.

Viewpoints: Some Aspects of Anglican Thinking. Edited, with J. B. Coburn. New York: The Seabury Press, 1959.

The Word Incarnate: A Study of the Doctrine of the Person of Christ. London: James Nisbet and Co., 1959; and New York: Harper & Row, 1959.

The Pathway to Believing. Indianapolis: Bobbs-Merrill, 1960.

Proclaiming Christ Today. New York: The Seabury Press, 1962; and Toronto: Oxford University Press, 1962.

The Christian Understanding of Human Nature. Philadelphia: The Westminster Press, 1964.

II. ARTICLES

"The Religion of the Incarnation," in *Theology*, xxiii (November, 1931).

"What Think Ye of Christ?" in *The American Church Monthly*, xxx (December, 1931).

"Christianity and the Ethical Problem," in *The American Church Monthly*, xxxi (March, 1932).

"The Liberal Catholic Movement," in *The American Church Monthly*, xxxi (June, 1932).

"What Is Liberal Catholicism?" in *The Christian Century*, xlix (October, 1932).

"The Finality of Christianity," in *The American Church Monthly*, xxxii (November, 1932).

"The Doctrine of Christ," in *The American Church Monthly*, xxxiii (March, 1933).

"Religious Work in the American College," in *The American Church Monthly*, xxxiv (August, 1933).

"The Symphony of Life," in *The American Church Monthly*, xxxiv (December, 1933).

"Professor Clement Webb's New Lectures," in *The Anglican Theological Review*, xvi (January, 1934).

"The Liberal Catholic Position," in *The American Church Monthly*, xxxv (March, 1934).

"Catholicism and Modernism," in *The Modern Churchman*, xxiv (April, 1934).

"Liberal Catholicism and the Eucharist," in *The American Church Monthly*, xxxv (June, 1934).

"Christian Friendship," in *The American Church Monthly*, xxxvi (November, 1934).

"Restatement," in *The Modern Churchman*, xxiv (December, 1934).

"Some Early Christian Theologians I—Clement of Alexandria, Saint and Scholar," in *The American Church Monthly*, xxxvii (February, 1935).

"Some Early Christian Theologians II—Tertullian," in *The American Church Monthly*, xxxvii (March, 1935).

"Dr. Bouquet's 'Modern Handbooks of Religion,'" in *The Anglican Theological Review*, xvii (April, 1935).

"Some Early Christian Theologians III—The Religious Quest of St. Augustine," in *The American Church Monthly*, xxxvii (April, 1935).

"The Organic Nature of Christianity," in *The Holy Cross Magazine,* xlvi (September, 1935).

"Unity in Faith," in *The Holy Cross Magazine,* xlvi (October, 1935).

"Unity in Worship," in *The Holy Cross Magazine,* xlvi (November, 1935).

"Unity in Life," in *The Holy Cross Magazine,* xlvi (December, 1935).

"The Doctrine of Christ to Chalcedon," in *The American Church Monthly,* xxxix (January and February, 1936).

"Catholicism with Freedom," in *The Modern Churchman,* xxv (March, 1936).

"The Devotional Poetry of Thomas Aquinas," in *The American Church Monthly,* xxxix (June, 1936).

"The Catholic Faith and Catholic Sociology," in *The American Church Monthly,* xl (July, 1936).

"St. Paul and Modern Christology," in *The American Church Monthly,* xl (August, 1936).

"Speech of The Rev. W. Norman Pittenger," in *The Modern Churchman,* xxvi (August-October, 1936).

"Christianity and the Mystery Religions," in *The American Church Monthly,* xli (February, 1937).

"The Doctrine of the Church," in *The American Church Monthly,* xli (March, 1937).

"The Epistle to the Galatians and Its Significance Today," in *The American Church Monthly,* xli (April, 1937).

"Some Thoughts on a Christian Philosophy," in *The Holy Cross Magazine,* xlviii (April-June, 1937).

"Paul Elmer More as a Theologian," in *The American Church Monthly,* xli (June, 1937).

"The Educational Process," in *The American Church Monthly,* xlii (October, 1937).

"Does Christianity Matter?" in *The Holy Cross Magazine,* xlviii (November, 1937).

"John Donne as Religious Philosopher and Theologian," in *The American Church Monthly,* xlii (November, 1937).

"The Notes and Authority of the Church," in *The Holy Cross Magazine,* xlviii (December, 1937).

"Axioms of Catholic Christology," in *The New American Church Monthly,* i (January, 1938).

"The Christology of the German Crisis-Theology," in *The Anglican Theological Review,* xx (January, 1938).

"The English Doctrinal Commission's Report," in *The Living Church,* cxxxviii (2 February 1938).

"A Word in Season," in *The New American Church Monthly,* 1 (February, 1938).

"Essays in Pastoral Care 5: The Aims of Religious Education," in *The Holy Cross Magazine,* xlix (March, 1938).

"Can a Man Save Himself?" in *The Holy Cross Magazine,* xlix (April, 1938).

"The Holy Eucharist," in *The Holy Cross Magazine,* xlix (June, 1938).

"Christianity and the 'Young Intellectuals,' " in *The Holy Cross Magazine,* xlix (August, 1938).

"The Revival of Scholasticism," in *The Holy Cross Magazine,* xlix (October, 1938).

"The Everlasting Gospel," in *The Holy Cross Magazine,* xlix (December, 1938).

"The Christian Doctrine of Salvation," in *The Anglican Theological Review,* xxi (January, 1939).

"Mighty Acts," in *The Holy Cross Magazine,* l (April, 1939).

"What Is the Holy Eucharist?" in *The Holy Cross Magazine,* l (June, 1939).

"Some Axioms of a Catholic Christology," in *Theology,* xxxix (August, 1939).

"America and the 'New' Theology," in *Theology,* xl (April, 1940).

"Conscience," in *The Anglican Theological Review,* xxiii (October, 1941).

"The Value of the Liberal Tradition in Historic Christianity," in *The Anglican Theological Review,* xxiv (October, 1942).

"Changing Emphases in American Theology," in *Religion in Life,* xii (Summer, 1943).

"The Church in Peril of Praise," in *The Christian Century,* lx (21 July 1943).

"The Spirit of Eastern Orthodoxy," in *Christendom,* viii (Autumn, 1943).

"The Church as the Body of Christ," in *Christendom,* ix (Spring, 1944).

"The Universal Doctor," in *The Anglican Theological Review,* xxvi (April, 1944).

"I Went to a Conference of Educators," in *The Christian Century,* lxvi (5 April 1944).

"Religion and the College," in *The Christian Century,* lxvi (5 April 1944).

W. Norman Pittenger—A BIBLIOGRAPHY   163

"What Is Disturbing Episcopalians?" in *The Christian Century,* LXVI (10 May 1944).

"Does God Make Any Difference?" in *The Christian Century,* LXI (23 August 1944).

"The Christian Philosophy of John Scotus Erigena," in *The Journal of Religion,* II (October, 1944).

"God and Our Troubled World," in *Christendom,* x (Spring, 1945).

"Biblical Religion and Biblical Theology," in *The Journal of the Bible and Religion,* XXXIII (November, 1945).

"The Catholic Church and Christianity," in *The Living Church,* CXII (1946).

"The Christian Hope of a Transfigured World," in *The Gospel, The Church and the World,* ed. K. S. Latourette (New York: Harper & Row, 1946), Vol. III.

"Origins of the Liturgy," in *The Anglican Theological Review,* XXVIII (January, 1946).

"Development versus Innovation," in *The Living Church,* CXIII (24 February 1946).

"The Realization of Empirical Catholicity," in *Christendom,* XI (Spring, 1946).

"Christianity Is a Culture!" in *The Christian Century,* LXIII (31 July 1946).

"Religion and Morality," in *Christendom,* XI (Autumn, 1946).

"God and the World: Their Relationship as Seen in Jewish Prophecy," in *The Anglican Theological Review,* XXIX (April, 1947).

"What Is Truth for Christians?" in *The Christian Century,* LXIV (25 June 1947).

"Man the Amphibian," in *Christendom,* XII (Autumn, 1947).

"The Earliest Philosophy of History," in *The Anglican Theological Review,* XXIX (October, 1947).

"Seed-ground for Leadership," in *The Christian Century,* LXIV (8 October and 19 November, 1947).

"Heaven Is My Home," in *The Living Church,* CXV (14 December 1947).

"Art and the Christian," in *The Christian Century,* LXIV (31 December, 1947).

"Anglo-Catholicism," in V. Ferm (ed.), *Religion in the Twentieth Century* (New York: Philosophical Library, 1948).

"Contemporary Anglicanism and the Challenge of Our Time," in *The Anglican Theological Review,* XXX (January, 1948).

"The Presuppositions of Religious Education," in *The Living Church*, CXVII (3 October 1948).

"Detachment versus Attachment," in *Religion in Life*, XVIII (Spring, 1949).

"The Church's Order," in *Theology* XLIX (April, 1949).

"Unity: The Problem of the Different Spirit," in *The Living Church*, CXIX (21 August 1949).

"The Theological Enterprise and the Life of the Church," in *The Anglican Theological Review*, XXXI (October, 1949).

"Compromise and Morality," in *The Christian Century*, LXV (30 November 1949).

"The Prophet Isaiah," in *The Anglican Theological Review*, XXXI (July, 1950).

"Community Life in Christ," in *The Living Church*, CXXI (29 October 1950).

"Devotion to the Mother of Christ in Catholic Spirituality," in *The Anglican Theological Review*, XXXIII (April, 1951).

"Christian Apologetics," in *Theology*, LV (1952).

"The Sacrament of the Lord's Supper," in *Religion in Life*, XXII (1952).

"St. Irenaeus," in *The Anglican Theological Review*, XXXIV (January, 1952).

"The Sacramental System of the Body of Christ," in *The Anglican Theological Review*, XXXV (April, 1953).

"What Is an Episcopalian?" in *Look*, XVII (19 May 1953).

"Reflections on a Holiday," in *The Christian Century*, LXX (2 September 1953).

"Theology and Reality," in *The Anglican Theological Review*, XXXV (October, 1953).

"Christianity and Americanism," in *The Living Church*, CXXVIII (January, 1954).

"The Hope of a Christian," in *The Living Church*, CXXVIII (7 February 1954).

"Rethinking the Christian Message," in *Religion in Life*, XXIV (Winter, 1954).

"The Problem of the Historical Jesus," in *The Anglican Theological Review*, XXXVI (April, 1954).

"Today's Theological Student," in *The Christian Century*, LXXI (23 April 1954).

"Putting Up with the Church," in *The Christian Century*, LXXI (27 October 1954).

"An Affair of the Will," in *The Living Church*, CXXIX (5 December 1954).

"A New and Catholic Modernism," in *Theology*, LIX (April, 1955).

"The Christian Apologetic of Franklin Bethune-Baker," in *The Anglican Theological Review*, XXXVII (October, 1955).

"What a Christian Ought to Know and Believe," in *The Christian Century*, LXXII (14 December 1955).

"Søren Kierkegaard," in *The Anglican Theological Review*, XXXVIII (January, 1956).

"Problems of Moods," in *The Living Church*, CXXXII (19 February 1956).

"Wanted: A New Christian Modernism," in *The Christian Century*, LXXII (6 April 1956).

"Reinhold Niebuhr," in *The Living Church*, CXXXII (6 May 1956).

"Need a Christian Be Afraid?" in *The Living Church*, CXXXII (13 May 1956).

"Christianity and the Man on Mars," in *The Christian Century*, LXXIII (20 June 1956).

"Degree or Kind? A Christological Essay," in *The Canadian Journal of Theology*, II (October, 1956).

"The Theologians and Science," in *The Anglican Theological Review*, XXXVIII (October, 1956).

"God's Secular Incognito," in *The Christian Century*, LXXIII (14 November 1956).

"Ersatz Christianity?" in *The Living Church*, CXXXIII (16 December 1956).

"Christ, the Church and Reunion," in *Theology Today*, XIII (January, 1957).

"The Church We Love," in *The Living Church*, CXXXIV (10 February 1957).

"Peace of Mind and Soul," in *The Living Church*, CXXXIV (31 March 1957).

"The True Social Gospel," in *The Living Church*, CXXXIV (9 June 1957).

"Religious Language: Some Proposals (on the Use of the Terms Myth and Mythological)," in *The Anglican Theological Review*, XXXIX (July, 1957).

"Knowledge: Theological and Ordinary," in *The Christian Century*, LXXIV (11 September 1957).

"The Three C's," in *The Living Church*, CXXXV (29 September 1957).

"James Matthew Thompson: Martyr of English Modernism," in *The Anglican Theological Review*, XXXIX (October, 1957).

"Augustinianism," in M. Halverson & A. Cohen (eds.), *A Handbook of Christian Theology* (New York: The Meridian Press, 1958).

"Catholicism," *ibid.*

"Some Important Contemporary Theological Issues," in *The Modern Churchman*, n.s. 1 (January, 1958).

"The Christian Understanding of Man's Sexuality," in *Theology*, LXI (July, 1958).

"The Significance of the Christological Question," in *The Modern Churchman*, n.s. 11 (July, 1958).

"The Christ of Our Christian Faith," in *Religion in Life*, XXVII (Fall, 1958).

"Doctrinal Report (of the Archbishops' Commission on Doctrine) and Anglican Theology," in *The Anglican Theological Review*, XL (October, 1958).

"Apologist versus Apologist," in *The Christian Century*, LXXV (1 October and 24 December, 1958).

"Theological Education," in *The Living Church*, CXXXVII (23 November 1958).

"Christianity and the Eschatological," in *The Anglican Theological Review*, XLI (October, 1959).

"In Defence of Universal Salvation," in *The Christian Century*, LXXVIII (7 June 1961).

"Paul Tillich as a Theologian: An Appreciation," in *The Anglican Theological Review*, XLIII (July, 1961).

"Preaching the Gospel Today," in *The Canadian Journal of Theology*, VII (July, 1961).

"The Christian View of Human Nature," in *The Modern Churchman*, n.s. v (October, 1961).

"Secular Study and Christian Faith," in *Theology*, LXV (February, 1962).

"Neo-Liberalism—Hope and Challenge," in *Religion in Life*, XXXII (Summer, 1963).

"Ernesto Buonaiuti and Roman Catholic Modernism," in *Theology*, LXVII (September, 1964).

"A Contemporary Trend in North American Theology: Process Thought and Christian Faith," in *Religion in Life*, XXXIV (Autumn, 1965).

III. PAMPHLETS

"Can a Man Save Himself?" West Park, N.Y.: Holy Cross Press, n.d.

"Christian Love, Hope and Faith." Cincinnati: Forward Movement Publications, 1956.

"The Church We Love." Cincinnati: Forward Movement Publications, 1957.

"Does Christianity Matter?" West Park, N.Y.: The Holy Cross Press, n.d.

"Is Christianity Final?" West Park, N.Y.: The Holy Cross Press, n.d.

"Jesus Christ God's Son Our Lord." Cincinnati: Forward Movement Publications, 1951.

"Living Christianly." Cincinnati: Forward Movement Publications, 1951.

"On Becoming a Christian." Cincinnati: Forward Movement Publications, 1956.

"Religion of the Golden Rule." Cincinnati: Forward Movement Publications, 1954.

"This Great Sacrament." Cincinnati: Forward Movement Publications, 1958.

"What about Jesus?" West Park, N.Y.: Holy Cross Press, n.d.

"Will There Be a New Religion?" West Park, N.Y.: The Holy Cross Press, n.d.

Contributors' Notes

W. Norman Pittenger—*An Appreciation*

1. Hardy and Pittenger (eds.), *This Holy Fellowship* (New York: Morehouse-Gorham, 1939), p. 37.
2. Pittenger, *The Approach to Christianity* (London: Centenary Press, 1939), p. vi.
3. Pittenger, *The Word Incarnate* (London: James Nisbet & Co., 1959), p. 284.

1   Israel, Pagan Culture, and Biblical Theology

1. The pioneer work on the subject was Martin Noth, *Das System der zwoelf Staemme Israels* (Stuttgart, 1930). Cf. also Noth, *The History of Israel* (2nd English ed.; New York, 1960), pp. 53-138.
2. This is the view of Noth, *ibid.*, p. 53.
3. Cf. John Bright, *A History of Israel* (Philadelphia, 1959), pp. 128-160. Different as Bright's conclusions are from Noth's, the formative role of the amphictyony receives equal stress. The same is true of the creative alternative view of Israel's origins proposed by G. E. Mendenhall, "The Hebrew Conquest of Palestine," in *Biblical Archaeologist*, XXV (1962), pp. 66-87.
4. Cf. Noth, *History*, p. 290. For an extremely negative judgment on Israel's postamphictyonic religious history, cf. the treatment of the Temple by G. E. Wright, *The Rule of God: Essays in Biblical Theology* (Garden City, 1960), pp. 59-76.
5. For a vigorously positive assessment of "non-Israelite" theological motifs in the Old Testament, cf. C. A. Simpson, "An Inquiry into the Biblical Theology of History," in *Journal of Theological Studies*, New Series XII (1961), pp. 1-13. For what is stressed in the present article, cf. particularly p. 3.
6. The biblical narrative of these events is found in I Samuel.
7. The kingdom of Eshbaal was never effective. (On the proper form of the name of Saul's son, cf. W. F. Albright, *Archaeology and the Religion of Israel* [Baltimore, 1942], p. 207).
8. Albrecht Alt, *Kleine Schriften zur Geschichte des Volkes Israel*, II (Munich, 1953), p. 41, and Noth, *History*, p. 181, postulate a previous six-clan Judahite amphictyony at Hebron. Cf. Murray Newman, *The People of the Covenant* (Nashville, 1962), pp. 138, 153. I should deem it likely that David himself had a good deal to do with the consolidation of previously disparate Judahite elements, and that Judah was familiar with traditions of kingship at Hebron even before the time of David.
9. The ambiguity of the situation may be read between the lines in the account of David's recognition as king by the leaders of the amphictyony in

II Sam. 5:1-3. Both Alt, *Kleine Schriften*, II, pp. 37-42, 129, who regards the reference in II Sam. 5:2 to David as *nagid* (older, amphictyonic leader) as fictitious propaganda designed to connect David's kingship with the older traditions, and Bright, *History*, pp. 174-177, who takes the reference to be an accurate reflection of the way in which David came to power, fail to recognize the complexity of the situation. What meant one thing to "Israel" (5:2) meant quite another thing to the Judahites and later monarchists (5:3). David's genius lay in his ability to hold both groups, and others as well, together.

10. The reference here is to I Sam. 4:21-22. In support of the argument in Section II of this essay, it is interesting to note that the proclamation in the Book of Ezekiel that restoration can follow judgment is related to the departure and return of "glory" to the Jerusalem Temple. Is the writer of I Sam. 4:21-22 locating the origin of Israel's eschatology just where this essay also locates it?

11. On the world in which Israel lived, cf. Henri Frankfort *et al.*, *The Intellectual Adventure of Ancient Man* (Chicago, 1946); W. F. Albright, *From the Stone Age to Christianity* (Baltimore, 1940); Albright, *Archaeology and the Religion of Israel* (Baltimore, 1942).

12. Given criticisms of British and Scandinavian scholars for "patternism" —cf. Henri Frankfort, *The Problem of Similarity in Ancient Near Eastern Religion* (Oxford, 1951)—it should be stated that in this one-paragraph sketch justice cannot be done to the variety in which a widespread and long-lasting culture manifested itself.

13. Cf. Babylon's mythos, the *Enuma elish*, in J. B. Pritchard (ed.), *Ancient Near Eastern Texts* (2nd ed.; Princeton, 1955), pp. 60-72.

14. On this credo, preserved in Deut. 26:5-9, Josh. chap. 24, and in the structure of the Pentateuch as a whole, cf. Gerhard von Rad, *Das formgeschichtliche Problem des Hexateuchs* (Stuttgart, 1938), and the introduction to von Rad's *Genesis* (Philadelphia, 1961).

15. For an excellent treatment of the way in which Israel consistently "demythologized" the myths present in her culture, cf. B. W. Childs, *Myth and Reality in the Old Testament* (London, 1960).

16. The covenant is used as the key concept in Israel's theology by Walther Eichrodt, *Theologie des Alten Testaments* (Leipzig, 1933-39); Eng. trans., *Theology of the Old Testament*, I, (Philadelphia, 1961).

17. Here the basic work is Alt's "Die Urspruenge des israelitischen Rechts," in *Kleine Schriften*, I, pp. 278-332.

18. Cf. V. Korosbec, *Hethitische Staatsvertraege* (Leipzig, 1931), pp. 88 ff., and G. E. Mendenhall, *Law and Covenant in Israel and the Ancient Near East* (Pittsburgh, 1955).

19. Cf. the way in which the older Sumerian culture and religion were appropriated by successive Semitic kingdoms and empires in Mesopotamia. Even the Philistines seem to have taken over the Canaanite traditions of the cities they captured: cf. Albright, *Archaeology and the Religion of Israel*, p. 220.

20. Cf. the article cited in note 3 above.

21. Cf. the traditions preserved in the Book of Judges.

22. The Old Testament traditions hint at one such move: Deut., chap. 27 and Josh., chap. 24, as well as other things, point to the centrality of Shechem,

but Shiloh is clearly central in the period treated in I Sam., chaps. 1 ff. Possibly the story of Abimelech in Judg., chap. 9, preserves the memory of the reason for the move. On the terminology for Yahweh's "dwelling" with Israel, cf. F. M. Cross, in *Biblical Archaeologist*, X (1947), pp. 65-68.

23. I Sam., chaps. 1-4. On the problem of the sources in I Samuel, cf. the various introductions and commentaries.

24. I Sam., chap. 11, is probably the oldest and most authentic tradition of Saul's emergence as a leader. Cf. Adolphe Lods, *Israel* (London, 1932), pp. 352-356

25. Cf. Noth, *History*, p. 169.

26. Cf. Jer. 26:6; Ps. 78:60 (English, 78:61).

27. On how the account of the fortunes of the ark from the beginning of the Philistine war until its establishment in Jerusalem was the *hieros logos* of the sanctuary there, cf. Leonhard Rost, *Die Ueberlieferung von der Thronnachfolge Davids* (Stuttgart, 1926), pp. 4-47.

28. For a sane presentation of the case for this, cf. Aubrey Johnson, *Sacral Kingship in Ancient Israel* (Cardiff, 1955), particularly pp. 27-46.

29. Cf. Absalom's subtle appeal in II Sam. 15:1-6, and the distinction between Israel and Judah in II Sam. 20:1-2.

30. Cf. I Kings 12:1 and what it implies, and Israel's cry in I Kings 12:16.

31. I have tried to give such an interpretation of this literature in *God and History in the Old Testament* (New York, 1960), chap. 2. It should be noted that to pass such a judgment on this literature is not to deny it inspiration or canonicity.

32. This is not to say that eschatology or "messianism" originated in David's time, but that what happened then, when appropriated, was its basis.

33. Ps. 78, whatever its date, also celebrates this. The same kind of thing is implicitly maintained in the narrative of the fortunes of the ark as interpreted by Rost. Cf. note 27 above.

34. Cf., for example, the implications of such a remarkable statement as Amos 9:7, which I would attribute to Amos himself.

35. For this reason, Bright's interpretation of the prophets misses a good deal. Cf. his *History*, pp. 247-248.

36. The literature on this subject is vast. Hugo Gressmann, *Der Ursprung der israelitisch-juedischen Eschatologie* (Göttingen, 1905), was epochal. Cf. also Sigmund Mowinckel, *He That Cometh* (Oxford, 1956), and Aage Bentzen, *King and Messiah* (London, 1955).

37. Again, the literature is vast. Johnson's *Sacral Kingship* may be referred to both for bibliography and for its own soundness of treatment. This work does justice to all that must have been mediated to Israel through Jerusalem, and the conclusions (pp. 127-134) do justice to Israel's own uniqueness.

38. Cf. Mowinckel, *He That Cometh*, pp. 270-279.

39. Cf. as the most obvious example of this Ps. 82.

40. For a strong statement of Israel's uniqueness against the background of the culture, cf. G. E. Wright, *The Old Testament against Its Environment* (London, 1950).

2   The "Prophet" in New Testament Christology

1. See, for example, R. H. Charles, *Religious Development between the
Old and New Testaments* (New York: Oxford University Press, 1948), pp.
64 ff.; J. Héring, *La royaume de dieu et sa venue* (Paris: Libraire Felix
Alcan, 1937), pp. 57 ff. Cf. S. Mowinckel (trans. G. W. Anderson), *He
That Cometh* (Nashville: Abingdon Press, 1955), pp. 280 ff. The word
"messiah" can be used more strictly to mean the anointed Ruler of Israel or
more loosely to designate the supreme eschatological figure, however conceived.
In this paper I shall often use the word in the latter, and less exact, sense.

2. The important references are: CDC 12:23; 14:19; 19:10 f.; 20:1;
1 QS 6:4-6; 9:10-11; 1 QSa 2:12-20. See also K. G. Kuhn, "The Two
Messiahs of Aaron and Israel" in K. Stendahl (ed.), *The Scrolls and the New
Testament* (New York: Harper & Row, 1957), pp. 54-64; M. Black, *The
Scrolls and Christian Origins* (New York: Charles Scribner's Sons, 1961),
pp. 145 ff.; "Messianic Motifs of Qumran in the New Testament," *New
Testament Studies*, III (1956-57), pp. 195 ff.; L. H. Silberman, "The Two
'Messiahs' of the Manual of Discipline," *Vetus Testamentum*, V (1955), pp.
77 ff.; H. Ringgren (tr. Emilie Sander), *The Faith of Qumran* (Philadel-
phia: Fortress Press, 1963), pp. 173 ff.

3. See, for example, Matt. 21:46; Mark 6:4, 15; 8:28; Luke 7:16;
13:33; 24:19.

4. O. Cullmann, *The Christology of the New Testament* (Philadelphia:
Westminster Press, 1959), p. 42.

5. The Synoptic Gospels clearly state that it was only "after John was
arrested" that "Jesus came into Galilee, preaching the gospel of God" (Mark
1:14). Jesus' ministry *followed* John's. In the Fourth Gospel a different
picture emerges: the two ministries run concurrently for a while. If, as seems
probable, the author of the Fourth Gospel was concerned with a rival John-
the-Baptist movement in his own time, there were some dramatic advantages
to be gained from the representation of Jesus and John themselves as having
been fully contemporaries. This concurrence makes it possible for John to pay
repeated tribute to Jesus as the Christ, to commend his own disciples to Jesus,
and to deny any rivalry: "He must increase, but I must decrease." (Cf. John
1:19-37; 3:25 ff.; 5:33 ff.)

6. The hypothesis that the early Christians were first responsible for
interpreting Elijah, or the Prophet, as the herald of the coming Messiah (as
distinguished from God's own coming in judgment) was stated, without any
attempt at demonstration, in my small book, *On the Meaning of Christ* (New
York: Charles Scribner's Sons, 1947), later republished as a part of *Jesus:
Lord and Christ* (New York: Harper & Row, 1958), pp. 231 ff. I ventured
to state this hypothesis because such exploration of the Jewish sources as I had
made had not disclosed any clear instance of the returning Elijah, or Malachi's
"Messenger," being thought of in any such way. I was very much aware,
however, that my explorations had not been exhaustive. I am the more grateful,
therefore, for an important section in J. A. T. Robinson's striking article, to
which I shall be making extended reference later ("Elijah, John, and Jesus,"
originally published in *New Testament Studies*, IV [1958], pp. 263-281, and
later in *Twelve New Testament Studies* [London: S.C.M. Press, 1962], pp.

35 ff.)—the section of the essay in which Bishop Robinson sets forth, entirely independently and with much more documentation, the same view. Cullmann (*op. cit.*, p. 23) seems to say that the conception of the Prophet as the fore-runner of the *Messiah* developed earlier and in a strictly Jewish milieu. Like Robinson, I have never been shown adequate evidence for this position, although it is commonly held among both Christian and Jewish scholars. Certainly I Enoch 90:31 and IV Ezra 6:26 (cited by H. M. Teeple, *The Mosaic Eschatological Prophet* [*Journal of Biblical Literature* Monograph Series, Vol. X, 1957], p. 5) do not make a convincing case for this view.

7. *Op. cit.*, pp. 38 ff.

8. It is hard to see how such a view could have been held in Jesus' own time, unless among persons far removed from actual contact with him and the events of his life (for example, Herod, to whom in fact the view is ascribed [Mark 6:14 ff.]). And if this idea of Jesus as John *redivivus* was either late or quite foreign to the Church itself, one may wonder whether the same may not be said of the other views mentioned in this connection (Elijah, the Prophet, "one of the prophets"). In that case, this passage in the Synoptics cannot be taken as evidence for primitive Christian thinking.

9. In the book of my own to which reference has been made (p. 231), I ventured to say that the "only clear case" of Jesus' identification with the Prophet was in Acts 3:22 ff., thus excluding the other passage, Acts 7:37. Actually in the latter we are told only that Moses promised a prophet—not who the prophet is, although his identity with Jesus may be considered clearly implied. In the earlier Acts passage, however, a far stronger case for the identification can be made. Still even this passage stops short of a forthright identification of Jesus with the Prophet. When Jesus is plainly named, he is called God's "Christ," "the Christ," and God's "servant" or "child." It is surely possible to read "a prophet from your brethren" (vs. 22) in close con-nection with "his holy prophets of old" (vs. 21) and with "all the prophets" (vs. 24). Looked at so, the whole passage is saying that the prophets of Israel, whom Moses likened to himself in authority, have without exception pre-dicted the coming of Jesus as the Christ. Teeple (*The Mosaic Eschatological Prophet*, p. 49) says concerning Deut. 18:15, 18: "Although this sounds like a reference to an individual prophet, the generally accepted view among Old Testament scholars is that the reference here is to the permanent institution of Yahweh's prophetic line. . . . This passage refers to the line of prophets." But if this was the original meaning, may it not have been the meaning also for Luke? I am not arguing that the conception of Jesus as himself the "prophet like unto Moses" is absent, even by implication, from this passage, but only that it is not as clearly present as has been commonly supposed. (But see the brief discussion of the "new Moses" idea later in this essay.)

If it be concluded, however, that the identification of the Prophet with Jesus is being made in Acts 3:22 ff., is it clear that Luke is not thinking of the risen Christ rather than of the earthly Jesus? Actually, if this is not true, the whole passage is curiously mixed and incoherent. For undoubtedly vss. 19-21 refer to Christ as risen and awaiting his return or the time of his "second coming." Can we be sure, then, that in vs. 22, the writer has the "first coming" in mind? The appearances of "raise up" in vss. 22 and 26 suggest—although they do not require—a reference to the resurrection. Commentators generally understand both verses in connection with the human career. Again

I am not meaning to take a contrary position, but only to point to the fact that the usual position is not clearly established. Ernst Haenchen recognizes the difficulties although he apparently has no doubt that they are to be resolved in the usual way (*Die Apostelgeschichte* [Göttingen: Vandenhoeck & Ruprecht, 1959], pp. 168 ff.).

10. *Op. cit.,* p. 38.

11. So far as Acts is concerned, I would understand Hans Conzelmann to be giving general support to such an explanation (*The Theology of St. Luke* [New York: Harper & Row, 1960], pp. 170 ff.), although this does not mean necessarily that he would regard the idea of Jesus the Prophet as relatively late.

12. W. D. Davies, *The Setting of the Sermon on the Mount* (Cambridge, Eng.: Cambridge University Press, 1964), pp. 25 ff.

13. In D. E. Nineham (ed.), *Studies in the Gospels, Essays in Memory of R. H. Lightfoot* (Oxford: Basil Blackwell, 1955), pp. 37 ff. On the place of Moses in the Gospel tradition see A. Descamps, "Moïse l'homme dans les évangiles et dans la tradition apostolique," in *Moïse l'homme de l'alliance* (Paris: Desclée et Cie., 1955), pp. 171-187. On Moses in Luke-Acts see also H. Conzelmann, *op. cit.,* pp. 166 f.; and S. S. Smalley, "The Christology of Acts," *The Expository Times,* LXXIII (1962), pp. 358 ff.

14. For the evidence at its widest possible see F. Hahn, *Christologische Hoheitstitel* (Göttingen: Vandenhoeck & Ruprecht, 1963), pp. 380 ff. Hahn would undoubtedly object to the distinction I am making between the "new Moses" and the eschatological "Prophet." He considers them together, along with many allusions to Jesus as "a prophet," and consequently regards "the Prophet" as both more primitive and more significant than it seems to me it was. The whole section of Hahn's valuable work that is concerned with "Der Eschatologische Prophet" (pp. 351-404) is most important. See also H. M. Teeple, *op. cit.*

15. See the article referred to in note 6 above, and also "The Most Primitive Christology of All," *Journal of Theological Studies,* NS VII (1956), pp. 177-189, reprinted in *Twelve New Testament Studies* (London: S.C.M. Press, 1962), pp. 139 ff.

16. For the best readily available accounts of the evidence for the existence and importance of this community see C. R. Bowen, "John the Baptist in the New Testament," *American Journal of Theology,* XVI (1912), pp. 90 ff., included in a volume of Bowen's essays edited by Robert J. Hutcheon, *Studies in the New Testament* (Chicago: University of Chicago Press, 1936), pp. 49 ff.; C. H. Kraeling, *John the Baptist* (New York: Charles Scribner's Sons, 1951), pp. 158 ff.; and C. H. H. Scobie, *John the Baptist* (London: S.C.M. Press, 1964), pp. 187 ff.

No attempt can be made in this essay to give an adequate bibliography on John the Baptist. The essay and books just named will mention much previous work. Among recent writings of significance I would cite especially W. R. Farmer's article on "John the Baptist" in the *Interpreter's Dictionary of the Bible,* and a work by Walter P. Wink, "John the Baptist and the Gospel" (1963), an as yet unpublished Th.D. dissertation at the Union Theological Seminary in New York. Each of these works has great value, both because of the critical attention they give to recent literature and for their own constructive suggestions. As regards the origin of the canticle, Luke 1:68 ff., Farmer finds it to be "Baptist"; Wink (pp. 201-206), Christian.

17. *Twelve New Testament Studies*, pp. 49 ff.
18. *Ibid.*, p. 50.
19. *Ibid.*
20. See in this connection Hugh J. Schonfield, *The Lost "Book of the Nativity of John"* (Edinburgh: T. & T. Clark, 1929). For a full and most interesting discussion of the birth narratives in Luke see R. Laurentin, *Structure et théologie de Luc I-II* (Paris: J. Gabalda et Cie., 1957), especially pp. 110 ff.; also P. Winter, "The Proto-Source of Luke I," *Novum Testamentum*, I (1956).
21. For Bishop Robinson the clinching argument that the canticle was originally composed to celebrate the birth of Jesus as both Elijah and the Christ is the appearance in it of the phrase "in the house of David" (vs. 69). There is no denying that the presence of this phrase makes a difficulty for the view I am defending. But it does so, at least in some measure, no matter how the question of original provenance is answered. If the canticle in the beginning had John in mind, how did this phrase get in, since John does not appear to have been of this "house"? But if it had Jesus in mind, why was it left in when the whole canticle came to be associated with John's birth, as it is in our Gospel? In view of the fact that Luke undoubtedly did some altering and adapting of the canticle as found in his source, whatever the source may have been, the presence of this phrase cannot be regarded as decisive either way.

3   Pistis Iēsou Christou

1. Some persons seem to have understood Paul to be teaching antinomianism, for he denies it vigorously in several passages (Rom. 3:8; 6:1 f., 15; etc.). The author of the Epistle of James also seems to have misunderstood Paul (see especially Jas. 2:14-26).
2. Cf. G. W. H. Lampe (ed.), *The Doctrine of Justification by Faith* (London: A. R. Mowbray and Co., 1954), pp. 22-27 and *passim*.
3. A full discussion of this difficulty may be found in Gottfried Quell and Gottlob Schrenk, *Righteousness* (London: A. and C. Black, 1954).
4. Cf. Rom. 3:22, 26; Gal. 2:16; Phil. 3:9; etc.
5. Stephen Ullmann, *Semantics* (Oxford: Basil Blackwell, 1962), pp. 156-160.
6. Cf., e.g., J. B. Lightfoot, *St. Paul's Epistle to the Galatians* (London: Macmillan and Co., 10th ed., reprinted 1892), pp. 154 f.
7. *Ibid.*, p. 155.
8. Walter Bauer, *A Greek-English Lexicon of the New Testament*, trans. by W. F. Arndt and F. W. Gingrich (Chicago: University of Chicago Press, 1957), *s.v. pistis*, 1, *b* and *c*.
9. Bauer, *ibid.*, 1, *a*; James Moffatt's translation of the New Testament; J. B. Phillips and NEB have "good faith"; Goodspeed has "integrity"; RSV, AV, and ASV have "faith."
10. Bauer, *loc. cit.*, RSV, NEB, ASV, Moffatt, Goodspeed, and Phillips; AV has "faith."
11. Bauer, *loc. cit.*, RSV, ASV, and Goodspeed; NEB, Moffat, and Phillips have "fidelity"; AV has "faith."

12. Bauer, *loc. cit.*; rsv, av, and asv have "fidelity"; Goodspeed has "good faith"; the others paraphrase.

13. Bauer, *ibid.*, 2, *d*, *δ*, and all the translations cited in the four preceding notes.

14. Or, more generally, in all expressions in which *pistis* is joined to a genitive (noun or pronoun) denoting Jesus Christ: Rom. 3:22, 26; Gal. 2:16 (bis), 20; Eph. 3:12; Phil. 3:9; etc. All of the English translations cited in footnotes 9-12 render *pistis* in these expressions by "faith."

15. So, e.g., Karl Barth, in *A Short Commentary on Romans* (English trans.; Richmond, Va.: John Knox Press, 1959), pp. 22 f.; T. F. Torrance, "One Aspect of the Biblical Conception of Faith," *Expository Times*, 68 (1956-57), pp. 111-114; and A. G. Hebert, " 'Faithfulness' and 'Faith,' " *Theology*, 58 (1955), pp. 373-379. The refutation of the arguments of Torrance and Hebert by James Barr in his *Semantics of Biblical Language* (London: Oxford University Press, 1961), pp. 161-205, is quite devastating; however, there are other arguments, as Barr points out.

16. So J. R. Mantey, "New Testament Words Inadequately Translated in English," *Bible Translator*, 2 (1951), p. 161, and Henrik Ljungman, *Pistis* (Lund: C. W. K. Gleerup, 1964), pp. 13 f., 37 f., 107.

17. J. A. T. Robinson, in *The Body* (London: S.C.M. Press, 1952), p. 63, fn. 1, seeks to interpret the genitive in *pistis Iēsou Christou* as subjective and objective at the same time; Adolf Deissmann describes it as a "mystical genitive" or a "genitive of fellowship" (in his *Paul*, trans. by W. E. Wilson; New York: Harper & Row, 1957, pp. 162 f.).

18. These illustrative examples are patterned after those of Eugene A. Nida in his *Toward a Science of Translating* (Leiden: E. J. Brill, 1964), pp. 59 f.

19. *Ibid.*, pp. 62, 65, 66.

20. I.e., all nouns x such that "John's x" implies "John has (an) x."

21. I.e., all nouns x such that "John's x" implies "John $V(x)$," where $V(x)$ is an intransitive verb with the meaning "perform x."

22. I.e., all nouns x such that "John's x" implies (a) "John $V(x)$ someone (or something)" or (b) "Someone (or something) $V(x)$ John," where $V(x)$ is a transitive verb with the meaning "perform x to."

23. If both types of transforms are possible these nouns may be called simply "transitive event-nouns."

24. I.e., all nouns x such that "John's x" implies "John is $A(x)$," where $A(x)$ is an adjective with the meaning "having the quality of x."

25. Leaving aside the possibility that "John's" represents "John is."

26. In the discussion which follows we shall, unless otherwise indicated, limit ourselves to the Pauline epistles, including Ephesians, but excluding the Pastorals.

27. We may, however, infer that *pistis* is an object-noun and that the genitive relationship is that of possessor to possessed in at least some of the occurrences of expressions like *hē pistis sou*, *hē pistis humōn*, etc.

28. The relationship does not, of course, have to be formal or etymological; thus, in English, "believe" is related semantically to "faith." In this essay, however, we shall limit ourselves to a consideration of words which are more or less obviously related.

29. I.e., roughly, a form which may be considered as the basis from

which all the related transforms may be derived. For a detailed definition of the kernel of a language, see Noam Chomsky, *Syntactic Structures* (The Hague: Mouton and Co., 1957), p. 45 and *passim*.

30. "Kernel" forms will usually be given with verbs in the third-person singular, present tense.

31. Forms of the latter expression occur in Acts 20:21; 24:4; 26:18; but not in the Pauline corpus.

32. It occurs as a variant reading in Matt. 27:42 and John 3:15, elsewhere with the accusative (e.g., as the usual reading in Matt. 27:42).

33. Since *hupo tou theou* belongs syntactically to *dedokimasmetha*, this conclusion is not absolutely forced upon us.

34. Cf. Polybius 5. 41. 2, 16. 22. 2 (cf. Liddell-Scott, *s.v. pistis*, III).

35. The meaning which *pistis* has in certain passages (especially Jude 3), i.e., "the faith" = "a body of truth to be believed," could, obviously, easily have developed from the meaning "trust" (= that which is entrusted).

36. In spite of the variant reading of A D* G *pc* it vg^{el}.

37. Cf. Bauer, *s.v. pistos*, and R. Bultmann, *Faith* (London: A. & C. Black, 1961), pp. 34, 60 f.

38. To facilitate comparison, these examples are cited in "standardized" form, i.e., here, with *pistis* in the nominative rather than in the accusative in which it actually occurs in Rom. 3:3.

39. I.e., *pistis* + the genitive of a noun other than *Christos, theos, Abraam*, or a synonym for one of these; e.g., *alētheia* (2 Thess. 2:13), *energeia* (Col. 2:12).

40. Where N is a noun other than *Christos, theos, Abraam*, or one of their synonyms.

41. See note 40, *supra*.

42. Not *pisteuei tini ti*, which has been discussed above.

43. This translation is, of course, supported in Rom. 3:3 by the fact that *hē pistis tou theou* is here contrasted with *hē apistia (tōn Ioudaiōn)*.

4   The Image of God and the Prosopic Union in Nestorius' *Bazaar of Heracleides*

1. G. R. Driver and L. Hodgson (eds.), *The Bazaar of Heracleides* (Oxford: Clarendon Press, 1925), pp. 166-167.

2. *Ibid.*, pp. 57-58.

3. *Ibid.*, p. 60.

4. *Ibid.*, p. 58.

5. *Ibid.*, p. 251.

6. *Ibid.*, p. 67.

7. *Ibid.*, p. 62

8. *Ibid.*, p. 63.

9. *Ibid.*, pp. 66, 59.

10. *Ibid.*, p. 75.

11. Cf. *ibid.*, p. 160.

12. Cf. *ibid.*, p. 157.

13. *Ibid.*, p. 55

5   Toward a Contemporary Interpretation of the
     Chalcedonian *Definition*

1. See, for example, H. R. Mackintosh, *The Doctrine of the Person of Jesus Christ* (New York: Charles Scribner's Sons, 1912), pp. 213 f.; W. Temple, *Christus Veritas* (London: Macmillan and Co., 1926), p. 134; G. L. Prestige, *Fathers and Heretics* (London: S.P.C.K., 1954), p. 146; P. Tillich, *Systematic Theology*, II (Chicago: University of Chicago Press, 1957), pp. 141 f.; H. W. Montefiore, in A. R. Vidler (ed.), *Soundings* (Cambridge, Eng.: Cambridge University Press, 1962), pp. 154 ff.; and W. Pannenberg, *Grundzüge der Christologie* (Gütersloh: Gerd Mohn, 1964), pp. 292 f.

2. P. Tillich, *Systematic Theology*, II, p. 141.

3. W. Temple, "The Divinity of Christ," in B. H. Streeter (ed.), *Foundations* (London: Macmillan and Co., 1920), p. 230.

4. W. Temple, *Christus Veritas*, p. 134.

5. See the full text of the *Definition* in, e.g., T. H. Bindley and F. W. Green (eds.), *The Œcumenical Documents of the Faith* (London: Methuen, 1950), pp. 191 ff. With this, compare Cyril's appeal to the Nicene Creed in his second and third epistles to Nestorius, which are edited in Bindley and Green, *op. cit.*, pp. 95 ff., 108 ff.

6. See R. V. Sellers, *The Council of Chalcedon* (London: S.P.C.K., 1953), pp. 208 f. The appeal to Nicaea was prominent also at the Cyrillian Council of Ephesus in 431.

7. E. Schwartz (ed.), *Acta Conciliorum Œcumenicorum* (Berlin and Leipzig: De Gruyter, 1932 ff.), II.1.2, pp. 126 f., 128; and P. Galtier, "Saint Cyrille et Saint Léon à Chalcédoine," in Grillmeier and Bacht (eds.), *Das Konzil von Chalkedon* (Würzburg: Echter Verlag, 1951), I, pp. 357 f.

8. It had already been sacrificed by Cyril himself in the "Formula of Reunion" of 433, as well as (slightly later) by the Patriarch Proclus in his *Tome to the Armenians.*

9. Cf. Leo, *Tome* 5 ("unitatem personae in utraque natura").

10. On the soteriological motivations of Cyril's anti-Nestorian polemic, a matter which lies beyond the scope of this discussion, see H. Chadwick, "Eucharist and Christology in the Nestorian Controversy," in *The Journal of Theological Studies*, N.S. II (October, 1951), pp. 153 ff.

11. On the occurrences of these expressions, see A. Grillmeier, "Die theologische und sprachliche Vorbereitung der christologischen Formel von Chalcedon," in *Das Konzil von Chalkedon*, I, p. 170 n.

12. Cf *Ep. II ad Nest.* (PG LXXVII.45C); *Ep. III ad Nest.* (PG LXXII. 116A-C); *De incarn. Unigen.* (PG LXXV.1220B); *Ep. I ad Acacium* (PG LXXVII.192D-193).

13. On the ambiguities of Cyril's language, especially his use of "nature," see R. V. Sellers, *Two Ancient Christologies* (London: S.P.C.K., 1940), pp. 95 f.; and A. Grillmeier, *Christ in Christian Tradition* (London: A. R. Mowbray, 1965), pp. 406 ff., 409 f.

14. On this point see Nestorius' estimate of the meaning of Cyril's terminology, in F. Nau (ed.), *Nestorius: Le Livre d'Héraclide de Damas* (Paris: Letouzey et Ané, 1910), pp. 267 f.

178 LUX IN LUMINE

15. For Cyril's use of this analogy, see for example *Ep. III ad Nest.* (*PG* LXXVII.116A).

16. *Ep. III ad Nest.* (*PG* LXXVII.100BC); cf. *De incarn. Unigen.* (*PG* LXXV.1212B).

17. *Ep. III ad Nest.* (*PG* LXXVII.112A).

18. *Ibid.*, 116C. The phrase is, of course, Apollinarian in origin and not, as Cyril thought, Athanasian. Cyril, however, uses it in his own way for his own purposes. The differences between his and Apollinaris' sense of the expression precisely define the gap between a classical Word-flesh Christology and Cyril's modified version of it, which we have called the "subject-attribute" Christology. See below *passim*.

19. Compare the remarks of Grillmeier, *Christ in Christian Tradition*, pp. 395 f.; and Sellers, *Two Ancient Christologies*, p. 95.

20. For another approach to Cyril's understanding of *hupostasis*, cf. J. N. Hebensperger, *Die Denkwelt des hl. Cyrill von Alexandrien* (Augsburg: Haas and Grabherr, 1927), pp. 94 ff. In my opinion this treatment looks for the wrong kind of profundity in Cyril's word-usages. In general (cf. Grillmeier, *Christ in Christian Tradition*, p. 410) it is enough to say that for Cyril *hupostasis* combines reference to the *reality* of a thing with reference to its being a particular *thing*. The *hupostasis* of Christ is thus "what (or who) Christ really is."

21. Cf. *PG* LXXVII.192D-193; 255D.

22. In Schwartz (ed.), *Acta Conciliorum Œcumenicorum*, I.1.6, p. 115.

23. See the revealing remark of Nestorius, in F. Loofs (ed.), *Nestoriana* (Halle: Max Niemeyer, 1905), pp. 197 f. "For what does [Cyril] say? [He says (cf. *PG* LXXVII.180B):] '. . . although the difference of the natures is not unknown, out of which we say that the ineffable union was made.' This phrase 'out of which' appears again! It is just as though, in regard to the natures of the Lord, he spoke of two separate parts, which [then] come together into one. For he should not have said 'out of which,' but '*of which* we say that the ineffable union was made.' "

24. For this idea see, e.g., *De incarn. Unig.* (*PG* LXXV.1221B); *Ep. I ad Succensum* (*PG* LXXVII.232D-233A); *Ep. II ad Succensum* (*PG* LXXVII.240BC); and Galtier, "Saint Cyrille et Saint Léon," pp. 368 f., with Sellers, *Two Ancient Christologies*, pp. 97 ff.

25. Cf. *Ep. II ad Succensum* (*PG* LXXVII.241AB).

26. On the sources of the *Definition*, see I. Ortiz de Urbina, "Das Glaubenssymbol von Chalkedon," in *Das Konzil von Chalkedon* I, pp. 391 ff.

6   Hegel's Logos Christology

1. There have been several important studies of Hegel in recent years, especially that of J. N. Findlay, *Hegel: A Re-examination* (London, 1958), and E. E. Harris, *Nature, Mind, and Modern Science* (London, 1954). Heidegger in *Holzwege* (Frankfurt am Main, 1957) also has a sympathetic study of Hegel's philosophy, although he thinks that Hegel had only an intimation of that truth which was to be fully developed in Heidegger's *Sein und Zeit*.

2. This was in fact the foundation for Hegel's own philosophy of history, and it is the method which he follows in the *Lectures on the History of Philosophy*.

3. Stirling, in his great book on Hegel, *The Secret of Hegel* (Edinburgh, 1898), quotes the following comment on Hegel's obscurity: "Who has ever yet uttered one intelligible word about Hegel? Not any of his countrymen—not any foreigner—seldom even himself. With peaks here and there more lucent than the sun, his intervals are filled with a sea of darkness, unnavigable by the aid of any compass, and an atmosphere, or rather vacuum, in which no human intellect can breathe. Hegel is impenetrable, almost throughout, as a mountain of adamant" (p. xxx).

4. Kierkegaard, *Philosophical Fragments*, trans. David Swenson (Princeton, 1936).

5. K. Barth, *Die Protestantische Theologie in 19 Jahrhundert* (Zurich, 1952).

6. All of these have been published and translated in one volume by T. M. Knox and Richard Kroner, as *On Christianity: Early Theological Writings* (New York, 1961).

7. See especially, *The Fragment of a System*, pp. 312 f.

8. Cf. the essay by G. Schrader, "The Philosophy of Existence," in C. W. Hendel (ed.), *The Philosophy of Kant and the Modern World* (New York, 1957), esp. pp. 49-52.

9. Hegel, *The Phenomenology of Mind*, trans. J. B. Baillie (London, 1949, 2nd ed.), p. 141.

10. Cf. Kierkegaard's analysis of despair in *The Sickness unto Death* (Princeton, 1941), p. 146.

11. *Phenomenology*, p. 143.

12. Hegel's phenomenological method involves not only a showing or demonstration of what the philosopher has himself thought, but even more importantly the reader is involved in a philosophic enterprise in which he becomes a part of the content. Cf. *Phenomenology*, p. 69.

13. This was perhaps the main reason for the development which the English school of Hegelianism took.

14. Hegel's analysis of negativity as implicitly involved in Western philosophy up to his time is still excellent; cf. his *Lectures on the History of Philosophy*. For a more contemporary analysis see, J. Wahl, *Le Malheur de la Conscience dans la Philosophie de Hegel* (Paris, 1951).

15. *Phenomenology*, p. 93.

16. *Ibid.*, p. 96.

17. *Ibid.*, p. 99.

18. *Ibid.*, p. 457.

19. *Ibid.*, p. 459.

20. *Ibid.*, p. 767.

21. Hegel has already analyzed this in his section on "The Unhappy Consciousness." For him this is man's existence in freedom.

22. *Phenomenology*, p. 758

23. *Ibid.*, p. 769.

24. *Ibid.*, see esp. p. 99.

25. E. Cassirer, *Philosophy of Symbolic Forms*, trans. R. Manheim, (New Haven, 1953-1957), II, p. 26.

26. *Phenomenology*, p. 758.
27. *Ibid.*, p. 767.
28. *Ibid.*, p. 760.
29. Kant, *Critique of Pure Reason*, trans. Norman Kemp Smith, (London, 1933), A 146.

7   The Conversion of *Diastēma* in the Patristic View of Time

1. Recent discussion has flowed from Cullmann's ascription of a "linear" view of time to biblical writers in his *Christ and Time*, trans. F. V. Filson (Philadelphia: Westminster Press, 1950). T. Boman's *Hebrew Thought Compared with Greek*, trans. J. L. Moreau (2nd ed.; Philadelphia: Westminster Press, 1960), pp. 123-183, is interesting as an attempt to substitute an existential for Cullmann's linear view. On the Hebraic use of "times" and related terms, see G. von Rad, *Theologie des alten Testaments*, II (München: Kaiser, 1960), pp. 112 ff. J. Barr's useful *Biblical Words for Time* (London: S.C.M. Press, 1962), pp. 30 ff., criticizes von Rad, but it seems hard to avoid the force of his argument. It is of course possible actually to live "in" time and to make statements which reflect its existence without having a conception of it in the classical and later sense; and it is with the origins of such a conception in Christian circles that we are here concerned. No reference is made here to a distinction between *chronos* ("time") and *kairos* ("critical moment") that is sometimes attributed to biblical writers. The very notion that these terms are understood in distinction from one another has arisen from an attempt to uncover a subtle conception of time which appears only at a later point. None of the writers with whom we are here concerned is, in any case, aware of such a distinction.

2. A partial list of these studies is contained in notes 9 *et seq.*

3. Athenagoras probably makes a direct allusion to Plato's treatment of time when he speaks of the cosmos as an instrument of music moving in well-regulated time (*Supp.* 16.2, cf. *Tim.* 41E). But his point is that he adores the God who fashioned this cosmic instrument rather than confusing it with its creator: once again time is not of interest in itself. We shall deal later with the philosophical association of time and cosmic motion which is indirectly reflected in the Christian writings of this period, but it must be emphasized again that such indirect references do not constitute serious theological consideration of the subject. As a look at any number of instances of the use of the term *chronos* will quickly show, Christians frequently used the word "time," as did Jews and Greek pagans, without intending to convey any special idea of its nature. A study of the term without reference to the importance of the subject of time as such in a writer's thought is of little value in itself.

4. Origen relates time to the physical cosmos in his *Hom. in Gen.* I.1 (cf. Philo, *De opif. mundi* X.36), but only with the barest of allusions. That is, Origen simply accepts the common association of time with cosmic motion in much the same fashion as his Christian predecessors. Origen's use of the biblical term *aiōn* ("aeon" or "age") is often made a point of departure for the discussion of his view of time, especially as regards its use in reference

to the possibility of further lapses of rational natures in succeeding "ages" in *De princ.* II.3.5. But what Origen does here is simply to interpret various scriptural passages (esp. Wisdom 13:9, Eph. 2:7) in such a way as to discover the notion of future lapses in the sacred text. So far as I can see, the motives which lead to his speculations regarding this matter have nothing to do with the question of time. They are profoundly related to his attempt to locate sin in the satiety, mutability, or finitude of the soul rather than in the circumstances of embodied existence; but the issue of temporality is just precisely one which is not considered. For a contrary view, see B. Otis, "Cappadocian Theology as a Coherent System," in *Dumbarton Oaks Papers*, XII, pp. 97 ff., esp. p. 119 n.

5. Virtually the only discussion of Methodius' relation to early Arian views of time is in Otis, "Cappadocian Theology," pp. 104n, 121n. The published studies of G. C. Stead relative to the philosophical background of early Arianism have not reached this point. It is hard to tell precisely what status Methodius wants to assign to the divine Word in the passages cited, and it may be quite as important for the understanding of his thought to suggest the possibility that he is unclear on the matter at this point in his career as to see here allusions to a carefully conceived doctrine. That the notion of the interval of time is present in Methodius' mind in his discussion of the Word in *Symp.* VIII.9 is suggested by the use of the term in a slightly different connection in VIII.14.

6. The views of Zeno and Chrysippus must be reconstructed from fragments and allusions in other sources. The fundamental notion of the interval of time is discussed in Simplicius, *In Aristot. categ.* 88Z, Arius Didymus in Stobaeus, *Ecl.* I.104-6. Sextus deals with the self-existence of the phenomenon in *Adv. Math.* X.218, as does Plutarch, *De com. not.* 41. Callahan deals with Platonic, Aristotelian, and Plotinian views of time in *Four Views of Time in Ancient Philosophy* (Cambridge, Mass.: Harvard University Press, 1948). The only extensive treatment of the views of the Hellenistic schools is still H. Leisegang, *Die Begriffe der Zeit und Ewigkeit im spätern Platonismus* (Münster i. W., 1913). Some of the most valuable remarks on these views are those found in studies of Patristic ideas of time such as that of Otis, already mentioned, and others cited later.

7. The clearest expression of Methodius' Platonic cosmology is in *Symp.* VI.1, where God, the Word, and the rational element in man are all set in contrast with the body as spiritual rather than physical realities. It is interesting to note that in *De res.* III.18.1-4 Methodius accepts the notion that the soul is material. Even here, however, God remains a Platonic spiritual being; and in fact Methodius comes to admit the materiality of the soul in the course of an effort to resolve the classic Christian Platonic problem of explaining the confusion of the rational element without reference to the body.

8. It should be noticed that in *De res.* II.25.8, quoted earlier, Methodius sees history as ending in an undifferentiated interval equated with the biblical *aiōn*. While there are certain parallels in Stoic remains to the idea of an undifferentiated time interval, the eschatological aspect of Methodius' teaching is unquestionably Christian in inspiration. For the bearing of this point on the perplexing problem of Methodius' notion of the divine Word as inhabiting a permanently undifferentiated interval of time, see above, note 5.

9. Gregory of Nazianzus' discussion of time (e.g., *PG* XXXVI.320B)

simply follows the views of Basil without any signs of interest in the problems which led Gregory of Nyssa to carry his own discussion in the direction indicated below. On the Cappadocian treatment of time, see Otis, "Cappadocian Theology," p. 109n; H. von Balthasar, *Présence et pensée: Essai sur la philosophie religieuse de Grégoire de Nysse* (Paris: Beauchesne et ses fils, 1942), pp. 1-10; J. Gaïth, *La conception de la liberté chez Grégoire de Nysse* (Paris: J. Vrin et Cie., 1953), pp. 168-172. The common Migne references are used throughout in referring to the Cappadocian writings, though the *Sources Chrétiennes* and Jaeger texts are used in quoting Basil and Gregory of Nyssa where available.

10. Otis, "The Throne and the Mountain," in *Classical Journal*, LVI, pp. 146-165; "Nicene Orthodoxy and Fourth Century Mysticism," in *Actes du XIIᵉ Congrès International des Études Byzantines*, II, pp. 465-484. The full shape of the Cappadocian conception of spiritual progress is treated in works by Balthasar, J. Daniélou, E. von Ivanka, and others. As Otis points out, the Cappadocian view is in many respects anticipated by Clement of Alexandria; but what Otis also shows is that the rejection of the mediatorial conception of the divine Word paved the way for the Cappadocians to reassert and elaborate the Clementine view in a quite new form. The difficulty which they faced was that their rejection of Origen's teaching regarding the mutability of the rational nature as the cause of sin—the only successful Greek Platonic Christian effort to avoid the association of evil with embodied existence—made it hard for them to explain the present circumstances in which the soul finds itself (see above, note 4).

11. Otis' *Cappadocian Theology* seems to me to stress the unity of Cappadocian views of time at the expense of the difficulties into which Basil is here led or the new departures which Gregory of Nyssa is consequently led to make in an effort to resolve them. On the latter point, see Balthasar, *Présence et pensée*, pp. 8-10.

12. Balthasar, *op. cit.*, pp. 8-10.

13. Gregory attacks Methodius as well as making use of him; and indeed in both of the works under discussion Methodius and Origen form his favorite set of false alternative positions: cf. *De hom. opif.* XXIX (PG XLIV.233D), *De an. et res.* (PG XLVI.124AB). However, Gregory's main attack on Methodius is, in each case, directed against Methodius' specific notion of the creation of the body prior to the soul; and in both works he follows Methodius' general definition of the issues posed by Origen's view of the fall and restoration of the rational natures. In a number of cases, the differences between *De hom. opif.* and *De an. et res.* are explicable as results of Gregory's reflection on anti-Origenist arguments originally adopted in whole or in part from Methodius and subsequently rejected or revised.

14. It seems to be the concept of the "image of God" as the perfection of the total rational creation which provides Gregory with his chief means of explaining the association of the whole creation with the delay required for the formation of the human plenitude (*De hom. opif.* XVI; cf. XXII *passim*). See R. Leys, *L'image de dieu chez Saint Grégoire de Nysse* (Bruxelles: Edition Universelle; Paris: Desclée de Brouwer, 1951), pp. 85 ff. The procreation of angels (see above) presumably requires a certain amount of time, though it takes place much faster than that of men. I am unable to locate in the LXX Daniel the passage on which Gregory bases his view.

15. I here somewhat hesitatingly disagree with both Otis ("Cappadocian Theology," p. 119n) and Balthasar (*Présence et pensée*, pp. 6-7nn.), who allege a Plotinian influence on the *essential* Cappadocian view of time. Such influence is certainly present in their treatment of the soul, and in certain moods the reader of their works is likely to suspect that this influence extends in some fashion to the question of the relation of time and the soul. But if the essential element in Plotinus' view of time is his rejection of the contemporary association of time and physical motion, the Cappadocians certainly do not follow him on this point. Moreover, it is precisely by asserting the importance of this association that they are able to remove temporality from the divine Word and that Gregory of Nyssa in particular is able to discuss the relation of the lapse of time to the perfection of the rational creation. If some sort of Plotinian influence is to be felt in the assurance with which the Cappadocians combine their assertion of the eternity of the Godhead with remarks on the eternal state for which rational creatures are destined, it is very hard indeed to find specific instances in which this influence concretely manifests itself. Balthasar's contention that the Plotinian treatment of time itself owes something to the Stoic time interval (*op. cit.*) is another matter.

16. Callahan, "Basil of Caesarea: A New Source for St. Augustine's Theory of Time," in *Harvard Studies in Classical Philology*, LXIII, pp. 437-454. Other important studies include Callahan's book already cited; J. Guitton, *Le temps et l'éternité chez Plotin et St. Augustin* (2nd ed.; Paris: Aubier, 1955); and G. Ladner, *The Idea of Reform* (Cambridge, Mass.: Harvard University Press, 1959), pp. 203-212. G. Quispel's article on "Time and History in Patristic Christianity," in *Man and Time* (Bollingen Series XXX.3), pp. 85 ff., is a great and inspiring treatment of the subject which contains various observations on Augustine but is not directly concerned with the definition of time before us.

17. Callahan, "A New Source," pp. 445-447.

18. On the relation of Augustine's and Gregory's views of time, see "A New Source," pp. 453-454, esp. notes 39-41. See also Professor Callahan's "Greek Philosophy and Cappadocian Cosmology," in *Dumbarton Oaks Papers*, XII, p. 56n. As Callahan indicates, the problems here are very complicated: indeed our brief paragraph must be regarded as nothing but the grossest sort of prophecy.

8 The Jungle of Jordan

1. Austin Farrer, *The Glass of Vision* (London: Dacre Press, 1948), p. 118.

2. Paul Van Buren, *The Secular Meaning of the Gospel* (London: S.C.M. Press, 1963), p. 200, n. 5.

3. *Ibid*

4. *Ibid.*, p. 188.

5. Cf. Austin Farrer's definition of prayer, "To pray is to give God back the mind of God coloured with our own." *Lord, I Believe* (London: The Church Union, n.d.), p. 17.

6. A. H. Armstrong and R. A. Markus, *Christian Faith and Greek Philosophy* (London: Darton, Longman and Todd, 1960), p. 8.

7. It is perhaps not irrelevant to note here that Gore's last recorded words were "Transcendent Glory." G. L. Prestige, *The Life of Charles Gore* (London: Heinemann, 1935), p. 533.

8. K. M. Carey (ed.), *The Historic Episcopate* (London: Dacre Press, 1954), p. 5.

9. W. R. Inge, *Vale* (London: Longmans, Green, 1934), p. 74.

10. G. L. Prestige, *Fathers and Heretics* (London: S.P.C.K., 1940).

11. As quoted by A. M. Ramsey, *An Era in Anglican Theology* (New York: Charles Scribner's Sons, 1960), p. 72.

12. *Ibid.*, p. 142.

13. W. Sanday and N. P. Williams, *Form and Content in the Christian Tradition* (London: Longmans, Green, 1916), p. 120.

14. Karl Barth, *Church Dogmatics* (Edinburgh: T. & T. Clark, 1936), Vol. I, Part I, p. 188.

15. London: Macmillan and Co., 1933, p. v. The lectures of which this book is composed were delivered in the University of Leeds during the spring term of 1932.

16. In *Journal of Theological Studies*, Vol. XXXVI, p. 414.

17. R. H. Lightfoot, *History and Interpretation in the Gospels* (London: Hodder & Stoughton, 1935), p. 225.

18. R. H. Lightfoot, *The Gospel Message of St. Mark* (Oxford: Clarendon Press, 1950), p. 103

19. *Theology*, Vol. XXXI, No. 183 (September, 1935), p. 171.

20. *Ibid.*

21. January 5, 1962, p. 11.

22. London: S.C.M. Press, 1963.

23. A. R. Vidler, ed. (Cambridge, Eng.: Cambridge University Press, 1962).

24. J. Heywood Thomas, *Paul Tillich: An Appraisal* (London: S.C.M. Press, 1963).

25. "The Church and the Memory of Jesus," in *The Christian Century*, January 17, 1962.

26. R. H. Fuller, *The New Testament in Current Study* (London: S.C.M. Press, 1963), p. 147.

27. Quoted from the syllabus of dogmatic theology which I prepared for the students of the General Theological Seminary, New York, between 1960 and 1963; readers will have observed my indebtedness to Dr. Pittenger, for whose constant help and encouragement I am deeply grateful.

28. A. M. Ramsey, *The Gospel and the Catholic Church* (London: Longmans, Green, 1956 rev. ed.), p. 146.

9   Love and Justice Are the Same Thing

1. *Esquire* Magazine, October, 1959.

2. Anders Nygren, *Agape and Eros* (London: S.P.C.K., 1932-39), 2 vols.

3. *Love in the Western World* (New York: Pantheon Books, 1956).

4. *The Mind and Heart of Love* (New York: Henry Holt, 1947).

5. *An Interpretation of Christian Ethics* (New York: Harper & Row, 1935); *The Nature and Destiny of Man* (New York: Charles Scribner's Sons, 1941-43), Vol. II, pp. 245 ff.

6. Cf. Brunner's *Justice and the Social Order* (London: Lutterworth Press, 1945), pp. 114-118, 125; and Temple's *Christianity and Social Order* (London: S.C.M. Press, 1950), p. 75.

7. Gustav Aulén, *Church, Law and Society* (New York: Charles Scribner's Sons, 1948).

8. *The Biblical Doctrine of Man in Society* (London: S.C.M. Press, 1954) p. 168.

9. Oliver C. Quick, *Christianity and Justice* (London: Sheldon Press, 1940), p. 25.

10. *The Theology of Culture* (New York: Oxford University Press, 1959), pp. 133-145.

11. *Love, Power and Justice* (New York: Oxford University Press, 1954), p. 79.

12. *The Destiny of Man* (New York: Harper & Row, 1960), pp. 106-107, 187-192.

13. *The Philosophy of Civilization* (New York: The Macmillan Co., 1960), p. 311.

14. Cf. esp. his *Church Dogmatics* (Edinburgh: T. & T. Clark, 1961), III/4, and II/2, p. 719.

15. Cf. Maritain's *Moral Philosophy* (New York: Charles Scribner's Sons, 1964), p. 81; and Haring's *The Law of Christ* (Westminster, Md.: Newman Press, 1963), Vol. II, pp. 98 ff.

16. *Gospel and Law* (New York: Columbia University Press, 1951), p. 42.

17. *Critique of Practical Reason*, trans. T. K. Abbott (London: Macmillan and Co., 1923), p. 176.

18. London: S.C.M. Press, 1964, p. 122. His view is refined in his *Life and Fire of Love* (London: S.P.C.K., 1964).

19. *Some Principles of Moral Theology* (London: Longmans, Green, 1920, 54), p. 43n.

20. *The Elements of Moral Theology* (London: A. & C. Black, 1947), p. 137.

21. *Jesus and the Word* (New York: Charles Scribner's Sons, 1958), p. 117.

22. Alan Richardson (ed.) (New York: The Macmillan Co., 1951), p. 134.

23. Philadelphia: Westminster Press, 1946, p. 163.

24. *Christian Ethics* (New York: Ronald Press, 1955), p. 438.

25. *An Interpretation of Christian Ethics*, p. 210.

26. *I and Thou* (New York: Charles Scribner's Sons, 1958), p. 14.

27. *Two Types of Faith* (New York: The Macmillan Co., 1952), pp. 69 ff.

28. *Law and Love* (London: S.C.M. Press, 1940), p. 144.

29. *Morality and Beyond* (New York: Harper & Row, 1963), p. 39.

30. *I and Thou* (New York: Charles Scribner's Sons, 1958); *Between Man and Man* (Boston: Beacon Press, 1955).

31. *Ut supra, loc. cit.*

32. Cf. Joseph Fletcher, *William Temple: Twentieth-Century Christian* (New York: Seabury Press, 1963), pp. 48, 308.

33. *Justice and the Social Order,* p. 116.

34. London: Lutterworth Press, 1937, pp. 328-329.

35. Two works here are illuminating: Will Herberg (ed.), *Four Existentialist Theologians* (New York: Doubleday and Co., 1958), and Paul E. Pfuetze, *Self, Society and Existence* (New York: Harper & Row, 1954).

36. *Jerusalem,* 55:59.

37. Quoted by Brunner, *Justice and the Social Order,* p. 117.

38. *Morals of the Catholic Church,* 26.

39. Leo Tolstoy, *On Life* (London: Macmillan and Co., 1934), pp. 97-98.

40. *Reason and Ethics* (Cambridge, Eng.: Cambridge University Press, 1950), esp. pp. 10-64.

41. *Christ and Culture* (New York: Harper & Row, 1951), p. 15.

42. Henry Davis, *Moral and Pastoral Theology* (New York: Sheed & Ward, 1943), Vol. I, p. 310.

43. *Morality and Beyond,* p. 39.

44. *Ibid.,* pp. 39 ff.

45. Chap. 3. Cf. also Chap. 3 in his *The Rule and Exercise of Holy Living. Works,* 10 vols. (London: 1850-52).

10   Music and Belief—Two Questions

1. K. Barth, "Wolfgang Amadeus Mozart," in *Religion and Culture: Essays in Honor of Paul Tillich,* ed. W. Leibrecht (New York: Harper & Row, 1959), pp. 61-78. Subsequent citations of Barth are from this source.

2. S. Antek, *This Was Toscanini* (New York: Vanguard Press, 1963), pp. 29, 60.

3. Cf. *The Catholic Encyclopaedia, s.v.* "Music."

4. H. L. Mencken, *Mencken on Music* (New York: Alfred A. Knopf, 1961), pp. 186-187.

5. *The Catholic Encyclopaedia, loc. cit.*

6. I. Stravinsky and R. Kraft, *Conversations with Igor Stravinsky* (Garden City, N.Y.: Doubleday and Co., 1959), pp. 141-143. Subsequent quotations of Stravinsky are from this source unless otherwise noted.

7. I. Stravinsky, *Poetics and Music* (Cambridge, Mass.: Harvard University Press, 1947), p. 142.